THE SURFER'S
TRAVEL GUIDE

A Handbook to Surf Paradise

Chris Ahrens

Chubasco Publishing Company

Chubasco Publishing Company
P.O. Box 697
Cardiff-by-the-Sea
California 92007

Manufactured in the United States of America

Cover design: Michael Cassidy
Cover photo: Rob Gilley

Wonderful things--weddings, graduations, retirements—are often celebrated in suits and ties. And yet how many, if any, wonderful things actually occur in such attire. Peel off the layers of societal pretentiousness, slip into a pair of old trunks, and head out to the truly wonderful world of surf. Time to live—save the suit to be buried in.

Jack and Dick Cross in the summer of 1930. Rick Cross collection.

*"The knowledge you get from school and
colleges is second-hand.
The know-how you get from the sea, and waves,
and water is new.
By all means get some of this type of knowledge."
— Tom Blake*

TABLE OF CONTENTS

DEDICATION

To my little family, the reason that I don't need this

book anymore.

Special Thanks To:

My wife, Tracy, without whom nothing, this book
included would get done, Paul and Joline, Susan,
Jean, yo mama, Michael Cassidy and Bob Hurley.

Dible

Introduction

North Shore of Oahu, 1966: As crowds increased, the talk grew louder about Maui and Kauai. There were even rumors of surf on Molokai and the "Big Island." When some Australians told us that there were empty, warm water point breaks in Queensland, we didn't believe them. All the small-wave riders (myself included) dreamed about was following Bruce Brown to Cape St. Francis. Fiji, Bali, Tahiti, Spain, Portugal, Brazil and Mavericks were, to my limited knowledge, uncharted territory. The general belief was that the surfing world was mostly discovered and that there was no place else to go. A prominent fantasy in that day was to take our foam boards back in time to about 1935, to surf Malibu. Now, you can do better than that.

Using the information in this book, you can take a modern surfboard to places that resemble pre-Spanish land grant California, where waves similar to Malibu gently peel down endless points. Or, you can travel to power zones where reef passes rival the North Shore, but without the crowds.

I have fond memories of uncrowded surf in Hawaii in the '60s. And while those days can never be repeated, they were not the best I have ever had. No. Within just a few years I had surfed other great spots and experienced fascinating new cultures. In some of those places surfing was so new that a surfer would draw an entire village to watch him paddle out for the first time in anyone's memory.

The world is young and alive, and open for you to have a look at, to jump into. Go see it. Ride some waves. Fall in love. Get hurt. Leave the only footprints on a beach that lead to a perfect point wave. Explore.

But you need not be like other explorers who came, saw, and left the place dirtier and poorer. The new conquistador does not leave the land smoldering, or the people ready to kill the next foreigner they see. He knows that the world is fragile, and he makes sure that things are always as good or better for his visit.

Prior to 1970, a well-traveled surfer might have been to Oahu, Maui, San Blas, France, New South Wales and Northern Baja. Few had ever surfed Costa Rica, Panama, North Africa, or even Northern California. Maybe a few dozen people had ridden Uluwatu.

By 1973, I myself was off to explore new surf spots. While I didn't get as far as some, I did have a few unique experiences in Micronesia where the local kids pelted my friend and I with rocks as we rode some little waves alone near a jetty. Later that evening we were invited to a big feast, which featured the delicacy, "fruit bat." Both the pelting and the feast reminded me of my first trip to Hawaii. We had not found a great surf spot in Micronesia, but I think that we were the first to ride it, and to name it. That being a fairly political time of my life, I tagged it "The Rights Of Man." Of course, the locals probably had a better name for it, and when we left, changed it to something like "Dumb White People Who Swim In Shark Home."

Anyway, being first, or thinking that I was first to a surf spot is one of the best things I've ever experienced in my 35 years as a surfer. With that in mind, I do not intend to blow the cover on anyone's secrets in this book. What you will find here instead of secret spots is a basic guide to 16 surf destinations. This book will help you to get there and beyond.

Like most of you, I have never used a guide book in my life. (I did actually own one once when my sweet mother sent *"Hawaii On $5 A Day"* to my brother Dave and I on Oahu . We had a good laugh because we were living for about half that amount.)

Floor space at "Animal Farm" in Maui at the

time was 10 bucks a week. A spot in "Mad John's Courtyard" at Sunset Beach was also dirt cheap. You could get a two-bedroom shack complete with rats on "Roach Road" near Waimea Bay for less than $90 a month. (Split six ways that comes to less than a day's rental for rollerblades at Mission Bay). Brown rice, a primary staple, was pennies a bowl. Fruit was free, and nobody owned a car, so there was no need for gas money.

A big treat was to go to *"Perry Boy's All-You-Can-Eat Smorgasbord"* in Waikiki. The cost: one dollar, for those who could afford it. Those who could not, waited below the balcony in the sand where sausages, and rolls were wrapped up in napkins and dropped to hungry hands. Dinner at *Lahaina Bakery* on Maui in 1969 was also about a buck. A stand-by airline ticket from Los Angeles to Honolulu was $75. Surfboards at that time cost about $125, and I was outraged in 1972 when Mike Hynson, then at the top of the heap, charged the unthinkable sum of $25 to shape me an Island semigun. There were no leashes, rashguards, scented surf waxes or phone-in surf reports. There were only these dots on the map with weird names that made you sick with surf lust.

Everyone on the North Shore, or in Waikiki, or Encinitas, or Huntington, or Byron Bay or Jeffrey's Bay had it made. Even the poorest among us could manage to get away for the winter. Still, the crew who came before us thought that the surfing world was ruined by the time that we took our turn at paradise. They had lived in tents, or converted army barracks, where they paid nothing for the privilege of having perfect surf at the front door. Pioneers like Trent, Curren, Noll, Muñoz, Downing, Kekai and Brown (Woody) were all good divers, so fresh fish was always on the table.

Before them it was mostly Makaha, and before that there was the absolute paradise of Waikiki. I'll never forget Donald Takayama telling how he would leave his surfboard on the beach over night without fear of it being stolen. Since then, the octopus arms of development have leveled, paved, ruined and built higher and higher until all that remains of old Waikiki are Rabbit Kekai and the Bishop Museum. Powerless to restore what was, the surfer's search continues.

After a failed attempt to move to the California-Oregon border in 1979, I returned to Southern California where my wanderings temporarily ceased. It was then that I decided to write this book. Then also, I ran into Kevin Naughton and Craig Peterson, '70s pioneers who had expanded our horizons by discovering waves in remote regions of Africa. As we spoke, we realized that cumulatively we had covered California, Oregon, Washington, Canada, Baja, mainland Mexico, Central and South America, four Hawaiian Islands, two coasts of Australia, both islands of New Zealand, parts of Fiji, some of Samoa, a lot of Europe and a chunk of Africa. By '70s standards, we were well-traveled.

I proposed the book idea to them. They liked it, moved into my spare bedroom, and we went to work, hitting the libraries, pulling together information on remote surfing destinations and confirming that we had missed far more waves than we had found in our hunt for surf. The world awaited discovery.

We studied maps, made outlines, wrote a few rough drafts, argued about titles. For reasons too numerous and boring to mention, that first book project fell apart, and we went our separate ways. Still, the idea of doing a surf-travel book never left me. For a long time, I was too broke, or, ironically, too busy chasing surf to get started again. From time to time I mentioned the book to friends. Some thought that it was a good idea. Most recently, one of those friends was Bill Bernard, co-owner of *Hobie Oceanside,* one of the world's most complete surf shops. Bill told his brother Richard, and soon there was a meeting, and then lists, and questions and sample chapters drawn up. Another friend, Gary Clisby, a former traveling ASP pro surfer, also encouraged the idea. Along with the Bernards, Clisby decided to back the project. We were off.

At one of the meetings, someone suggested that we disclose secret spots. That was something that Kevin, Craig and I had agreed upon originally—no naming of secrets! We never did trust those who had practiced such treachery, and we wanted to leave the naming of the surf spots to the reader.

So, while you will not find many specific surf spots in this book, you will find it a priceless resource in helping you to get started in your search. It will point you to the best surfing regions in the world, and provide you with the tools for getting there safely. It will help to maximize your enjoyment once you've made the commitment to go. If followed, this book can save you thousands of dollars, a great deal of time and countless headaches. It will show you, as it did us a decade and a half ago, that the most familiar is often the most elusive. It will also show you that we are surrounded by a world of surf.

Like many of you, I have been to Hawaii numerous times, yet until I did my research I had no idea that there were more than a dozen places to camp for free on Oahu. I didn't know that there were over 5,000 youth hostels around the world, some near world-class surf spots, where you can stay in relative comfort for a fraction of the price of a hotel. I didn't know that there were ways to fly for nearly nothing, to some of the most desirable spots on earth. I didn't realize that a book of coupons could cut the cost of a good hotel on Maui nearly in half.

Well, now I know. And now, so will you. Follow this guide, but don't be afraid to go beyond it, off the path. There, you may have adventures which you previously thought only existed in books or movies.

Then, when you return home from your travels and someone tells you that all the good surf spots have been discovered, you will just smile and nod in the same way that Kevin and Craig have been doing for decades.

Happy hunting,

Chris Ahrens

Prices for travel and lodging in this book are aimed at the person who would rather surf all day in paradise and stay in a clean, comfortable hostel, over those who prefer to lay around in satin sheets in some expensive hell hole.

GENERAL INFORMATION

The following section is one of the most important in the entire book. It will tell you how and where to shop for discount airfares and lodging, where to contact your consulate and generally how to keep your surf paradise from becoming a living hell. Read it carefully, and **read it first**. It can save you a lot of time and money. While the following tips are general, many of them apply to every place you want to be.

AIR TRAVEL

Round the World Tickets often have numerous restrictions, but can give you stops like Fiji for about the same amount as admission for two to Disneyland, minus the mouse ears. Check with your travel agent.

Circle Pacific Tickets can get you some bitchin' stopovers for about $50 each. Ask your travel agent, and if she ain't cool, ditch her for another.

Visit South Pacific Passes are greatly reduced fares, but some restrictions do apply. Contact your travel agent, or contact:
Air Promotion Systems
5757 W. Century Blvd. #660
Los Angeles, CA 90045
Phone: (800) 677-4277
Fax: (310) 338-0708

COMPUTERIZED FLIGHT SCHEDULES

Please keep in mind that some of the phone numbers in this book are subject to change. Information on 800 numbers can reached by dialing: (1-800) 555-1212.

ABC Worldwide Hotel and Travel Guide:
(617) 262-5000
Easy Sabre: (800) 433-7556 x 4813
OAG Electronic Edition: (800) 323-3537
TWA Travelshopper: (800) 892-1011

Jet Lag: Set your clock to the time zone to which you are traveling. Live by that schedule for a couple of days, if possible. If that's not possible, set your clock when you get on the plane. If it's 10 p.m. at your destination, pull a blanket over your head and go to sleep. If it's 7 a.m. there, have breakfast. In short, try to hold to your normal routine using the time at your destination. Drink plenty of water. Avoid caffeine, sugar and alcohol. Since using this method on flights of up to 18 hours, I have never suffered from jet lag.

Aloha Airlines: (800) 367-5250
American Airlines: (800) 433-7300
Continental Airlines: (800) 525-0280
Delta Airlines: (800) 221-1212 or (800) 843-9378
Lacsa Airlines: (800) 225-2272
Mexicana: (800) 531-7921
Northwest Airlines: Domestic - (800) 225-2525
International: (800) 447-4747
Pan American Airways: (800) 221-1111
Qantas: (800) 227-4500
Transworld Airlines (TWA): Domestic: (800) 221-2000
International: (800) 892-4141
United Airlines: (800) 241-6522

Tip: Shop around. When one airline drops their price, you can usually get the same price from another airline.

Travel Naturally. Staying healthy on the road can be difficult. Try some of the following supplements:

- Ginger capsules are reputed to help fight nausea and motion sickness.
- Garlic is a natural antibiotic. We suggest the odorless capsules for obvious reasons.
- Grapefruit seed extract is another good, natural antibiotic.
- Enchiacea helps to boost the immune system, and is often combined with golden seal in capsule form.
- You'll still want mosquito netting, but a few drops of eucalyptus oil will hold off some of the invaders until reinforcements arrive.
- Calendula oil is good for cuts, burns, abrasions and rashes.

Major airlines offer as much as 18 alternative meals. Kosher, Hindu, vegetarian and low cholesterol are among the choices. Call your airline in advance to order your meal.

COMPLAINT DEPARTMENT

Better Business Bureau: (listed in white pages) Regulates operators and agencies in your area.

U.S. Department of Transportation Consumer Affairs Office: (202) 366-2220. Call them if you have problems with airlines.

Federal Aviation Administration (FAA) Consumer Hotline: (800) 322-7873. For carry-on baggage problems and airport security.

Safety Hotline: (800) 255-1111. Reports safety problems with planes.

U.S. Department of Transportation Consumer Affairs Office: (202) 336-2220.

MAJOR CONSUMER AIR TRAVEL PERIODICALS

Airline Passenger Services: (310) 493-4877. Cost: $75 per year.

Best Fares: (800) 635-3033. Cost: $68 per year.

Consumer Reports Travel Letter: (800) 234-1907. Cost: $37 per year.

Frequent Flyer: (800) 323-3537 x 0652. Cost: $52 per year. Free with OAG *Pocket Flight Guide* subscription.

IntelliTravel is a comprehensive PC software program on travel by AAA. Combines street and freeway maps with detailed listings of hotels, restaurants, campgrounds, and a guidebook. Order by calling (800) 513-7222 for $19.95 plus *S&H*. Ten dollars more for non-AAA members.

Helpful Associations For Students,
and even some young drop outs:

GO25 Card. Discounts on travel and associated stuff. Sold at student travel offices and some YHAs. For more information contact: FIYTO, Bredgade 25 H, 1260 Copenhagen K, Denmark.

ISTC. Special range of travel services for the international student and youth. Contact: ISTC, Box 9048, DK 1000 Copenhagen, Denmark.
Phone: (45) 339-39303/Fax: (45) 339-37377.

The Student Air Travel Association (SATA) offers discounts on air fares. Distributed by student travel centers.

The Explorer Pass offers up to one month unlimited and cheap rail travel on participating rail networks.

Distributed by **International Student Rail Association (ISRA)**. (Information available at student travel offices.)
The International Association for Educational and Work Exchange Programs (IAEWEP). Work exchange programs for youth and students.
STA Travel: (415) 391-8407

The International Student Identity Card (ISIC). For full-time students. Special prices on travel and travel-related things like 24-hour worldwide emergency service for card holders. Distributed by student travel centers, student unions and some national YHA's.

Tip: Pursue the cheap flight ads in the back of the Sunday newspaper "travel section."

Student fares: Check for student fares at college bulletin boards, tourist offices, student/youth travel brochures. Contact: *U.S. Student Travel Service,* 801 Second Avenue, New York, NY 10017. *Council on International Education Exchange,* 205 East 42nd Street. New York, NY. 10017. *AFS International/Inter-cultural Programs,* 313 E. 43rd Street, New York, NY 10017.

Fear of Flying?

Some private organizations and some airlines offer various seminars and programs to overcome fear of flying . Try: *THAIRAPY*: 4500 Campus Road, Newport Beach, CA 92260.
Fly Without Fear: 310 Madison Avenue, New York, NY 10017
Fearless Flyer Seminar: Pan Am, Pan Am Building. New York, NY 10017

Bartering for seats: Since deregulation, airlines will sometimes barter for seats if you can prove you can promote travel on their lines.

Some carriers that are not affiliated with the *International Air Transportation Association* can save you money. Ask your travel agent.

Free Travel?

Cargo Planes are perhaps less safe than commercial airlines, but they can provide a free ticket. Try remote airstrips. Ask for the captain of the airfield or go to the office of the cargo company. Schedules are uncertain, and there are no free beer nuts. Sometimes you can get free flights with the military, especially in Latin America, and especially if you are an attractive woman.

Courier services are legitimate organizations. You are not allowed any luggage, but carry-on. They want you to dress nicely, and deliver their documents safely at their destination. In return, you can receive greatly reduced or even free airfare. *Travel United Unlimited*, P.O. Box 1058, Allston, MA 02134, publishes a monthly list of courier flights. A subscription costs U.S. $25 or, call Now Voyagers: (212) 431-1616.

Tip: Not all air fares are equal. Prices vary greatly. Shop around.

Tip: Peak seasons for travel holidays and weekends, will almost always cost more. If you are not in a hurry or on a tight schedule, you can save lots of money. Book flights in advance to save even more.

Some Possible Discount Flights

Access International
101 W. 31st Street, Suite 104,
New York, NY 10001
Phone: (800) Take Off

Airkit
1125 W. 6th St.
Los Angeles, CA 90017
Phone: (213) 957-9304

Bay Area Travel
Phone: (800) 999-1938

Council Travel
205 E. 42nd St.
New York, NY 10017
Phone: (212) 616-1430
312 Sutter St., Suite 407,
San Francisco, CA 94108
Phone: (415) 421-3473

Discount Club America
6133 Woodhaven Blvd.
Rego Park, New York 11374
Phone: (718) 335-9612

Discount Travel International
Ives Bldg., 114 Forest Ave.
Suite 205, Narbeth, PA 19072
Phone: (800) 221- 8139

Inter World
3400 Coral Way,
Miami, FL 33145
Phone: (305) 443-4929

Nouvelles Frontieres
12 E. 33rd St.
New York, NY 10016
Phone: (212) 779-0600

Stand Buys
311 W. Superior St.
Chicago, IL 60610
Phone: (800) 331-0257

Travelers' Advantage
49 Music Sq.
Nashville, TN 37203
Phone: (800) 548-1116

Worldwide Discount Travel Club
1674 Meridian Ave.
Main Beach, FL 33139
Phone: (305) 534-2082

Phone: (800) Fly Cheap

Phone: Addis (800) 924-7359

Flight Savers
Phone: (800) 683-1233

 (800) Cheap Air
G. Franklin Travel
For free brochure, send SASE to:
P.O. Box 17712, IN 46227

Hawaiian Air Vacations:
Phone: (800) 353-5393

Pleasant Hawaiian Holidays:
Phone: 800-2-HAWAII

Jet Vacations:
Phone: (800) JET-0999

Cut Throat Travel Outlet
Phone: (800) 642-TRIP

Consolidator Discounts
Phone: (800) 576-7770

All Continents Travel
Phone: (800) 368-6822

Cheap Seats
Phone: (800) 451-7200

Cheap Tickets, Inc.
Phone: (800) 377-1000

Tip: Shop the *Cyberspace Highway (Internet, Compuserve)* for travel bargains.

Tip: Airlines often overbook flights. Don't worry, be happy if you are bumped. Many passengers have reported receiving free airline tickets to Hawaii or Costa Rica in order to compensate for the minor inconvenience.

PACKING

Packing Surfboards
The following tip comes from Gary Clisby, a pro surfer who has logged thousands of air miles in pursuit of waves.

Before packing, keep in mind that the airlines claim responsibility for lost baggage only, not damaged baggage.

If you plan on taking a few surf trips each year, get a good board bag. Consider the length of the boards you will be traveling with. Some shops have begun renting board bags.

Another option is a board box. Most surfers using boxes are packing guns to Hawaii. The boxes usually last only a couple of times before being reduced to a mass of mushy cardboard.

Whether box or bag, try to pack boards close together, protecting the fins and tail area. This keeps boards from shifting and damaging each other. It also makes the bag look smaller, and since the airlines can charge you per board, it can save you a lot of money. Also, the strength of two or more boards together reduces the chance of a board getting broken by the airlines.

For extra care, secure the trailing fin by wrapping packing tape around the tail and fin. For boards with fin boxes, remove the fins for travel, then tape in a towel or a piece of clothing around the tail area. Make sure to fill the space between the fins. Surf shops sell foam blocks designed to protect fins and tail area. Foam blocks work well, but they seem to take up too much space when traveling with three or more boards. Next, slip a board sock over each board. If you still desire more protection, you could wrap each board with bubble pack.

Now place the boards in the bag. Arrange the boards so that decks face out and the fins are on opposite sides. For more than two boards, place the longest board on the outside. This seems to insure good protection of fins and board bottoms. Now, with your boards fit closely together, zip the bag shut. Using tape or light rope, secure the entire bag with the straps on the outside of the bag. Put tape around the entire bag to keep the boards from shifting.

I have watched Rabbit Bartholomew travel the

European leg of the A.S.P. tour without a board bag for his two boards. He seemed to do fine by just taping his boards together and slapping on a luggage tag. In contrast, I have carefully packed my boards only to find the fins crushed through the bottoms. The airlines will put some dings in your boards, but you can put the odds in your favor by packing correctly.

Packing Check List

The following is a general list. Some of the items apply to places you are going; some don't.

- International Driver's License: Available at AAA for a fee of $10. You will need two passport-type photos.
- Passport: A valid passport application can be obtained through selected post offices. Check with them for requirements, or contact the Wash - ington DC Passport Agency at (202) 647-0518.
- Visas: Sometimes visas are unnecessary. They can usually be arranged through your travel agent. Try to get as long a stay as possible in one country. If you want to stay a while, request a multiple-entry visa from the appropriate consulate. This will entitle you to much more time in the country, and only requires spending about a day out of the coun try to get your visa stamped, before returning again. Do not, however, abuse the system, by trying to use this visa as residency. Local authorities tend to frown on such practices.
- Two or more leashes: Get leashes that are appropri- ate to the types of waves you intend to ride.
- First-aid kit: Good kits are available in many places. Check "General Information" for the ones sold at the *Magellan's* store. If you are going to a Third- World country try to bring a clean, sterile needle

and hospital-quality thread.

- Vitamins: It could be a while before you get a decent meal, and the fast-food circuit of multiple airports can really deplete you quickly.
- Thin booties (for warm climates with reefs).
- Goggles for regions like Bali where the sun tends to be intense. "Spex" is a good product.
- Waterproof sunscreen with an SPF of at least 15.
- Plenty of wax appropriate to the water temperature of your destination.
- Rashguard (long-sleeve if the sun is severe in the region you are traveling to.)
- Major credit card. Most places won't rent a car without one.
- Address book with numbers of nearest relatives, friends, bank, and all important numbers, including that of someone most likely to send you money in a pinch.
- Photocopies of all important documents. (Keep these separate from the original documents.)
- Portable water purifier (*Aqua Pure* makes a good one, and is available in many camp stores.)
- Small flashlight that can fit on a key chain, with extra batteries. Large flashlight with extra batteries. Several boxes of matches, a good knife. Two rolls of duct tape.
- Mosquito netting, coils, and repellent.
- The most detailed map of the area you can get.
- A hat that can be thrown into a bag without being ruined. *Made-In-The-Shade* makes a cap that you can wear in the water.
- Good sunglasses.
- Snorkel and mask.
- Ding-repair kit. *Solarez* is a good product for minor dings. *Neo Rez* is an instant wetsuit-repair kit

in a tube. For more serious dings, consider something like *Big Swell Ding Repair.*

- Backpack
- Lightweight tent
- Lightweight sleeping bag
- Lantern
- Stove. For international travel, *Adventure 16* suggests either the *270 Micro* by *Gaz* or a similar model by *Epigas.* Both are lightweight and operate on propane/butane canisters which are available all over the world. Cost: between $35 and $40.
- dried food
- ear plugs
- Water proof watch
- A good pair of slaps
- Magnetic hide-a-key
- Soft surf racks. Also, *Thule* makes tie-down straps, which some people consider more versitle than soft racks.

Tip: A good board bag can double, temporarily, as a sleeping bag.

GROUND TRANSPORTATION

The big cities are usually the best places to find **cars for sale.** Try to locate an area with a lot of travelers. The bulletin boards around the backpackers stops are good. If someone is leaving and wants to sell their car, you may be able to pick it up cheap.

Tip: If you're in Australia, New Zealand, South Africa, England, or anyplace where they drive on the left side of the road, it's a good idea to practice driving on one of the small country roads.

New Product: *Wheele.* If you are going to a place like the North Shore of Oahu, where the surf is all concentrated in one place, you might want to consider bringing a bicycle and a surfboard carrier. Try *Wheele.* It comes in sizes to carry bodyboard to longboard, and has a place to stash towels, wetsuits and other gear. If all surf-related items were designed as well as *Wheele*, there never would have been a recession in our sport. Call (714) 361-5800.

Tip: As many travelers in the U.S. can tell you, a AAA Card can be an extremely helpful item on the road. Not only will they tow your car, break into it for you if you lock yourself out, and bring you gas if you're stranded, now AAA offers discounts on car rentals and some airfares. Call (800) AAA - 5000 for more information. National Headquarters: 1000 AAA Drive, Heathrow, FL 32746. Phone: (407) 444-7000.

Tip: This one comes from an unlikely source, John Steinbeck's, *"Travels With Charley."* I've never tried it, but if it's good enough for Steinbeck... Anyway, the master writer says that if you secure a trash can in the back of the camper, fill it with water, dirty clothes and detergent, and drive for a few hundred miles, the clothes will come out clean. To rinse, drain soapy water, pour in fresh water, and keep driving.

Tip: If you plan on doing a lot of traveling, you will most likely need an **International Driver's License**. Not only is this document acceptable in most foreign countries, it will also make you feel really cool just having it. An International Driver's License can be obtained from AAA for $10. You will need to show a valid U.S. Driver's License, plus two passport-sized photos. The license is good for one year.

Tip: Have a good hiding place for your car key, and never let anyone see where you are hiding it. P.S. On top of the wheel is the first place they look. Try a magnetic hide-a-key device.

MISCELLANEOUS

Most surf-related items can be purchased cheaper in the continental U.S. than elsewhere. In fact, things like used surfboards (preferably a well-advertised brand) can even yield a decent profit when sold in some countries. Make sure and check beforehand if the country you are entering will allow you to sell your used boards or not. Some countries check boards in and out at customs. If you enter the country with a board and try to leave it without one, you could be charged duty. You will also find that things like leashes, T-shirts, and Levis are far less expensive in the continental U.S. than elsewhere. These make great gifts when traveling abroad. Make sure that new clothing always looks like part of your own luggage. If customs officials think that you are bringing in clothes to sell, they might charge you duty on them. Anywhere you travel, bring some sort of gift.

Tip: Shop where the locals shop.

Guard your passport. Some foreign passports are worth thousands on the black market in some countries. For an immediate temporary replacement, contact your embassy or consulate as soon as you find the document missing.

Tip: Get **travel insurance**. Your travel agent will advise you.

Tip: Don't buy ivory, turtle shells, or any other products made from endangered species.

Tip: Don't be an "ugly" American, Australian, or any other "n". Unless your name is Don Rickles, loud people who complain a lot are usually not welcome anywhere.

New product: Called the *Solar Capsule Cooker,* this handy little item cooks food, and heats water with no other power source than the sun. Haven't checked it out myself, but it could be a good one. *Solar Capsule* inventor Byron Cowart claims that he puts his food into the capsule, paddles out, and when he comes in, dinner's done. For more information, call Byron at (619) 728-5254.

Tip: Many countries around the world restrict travel on the basis of appearance. A neat appearance always works the best. Countries will restrict entry for two reasons: One, to prevent the entry of persons whose dress or appearance offends the local people. Two, to avoid admitting travelers who are likely to become destitute or stranded in their country. Hey, it's their country.

Tip: Make sure that your passport does not expire before your scheduled return. Some countries require that your passport be valid for six months after arrival. Get all of your documents— shots, etc.—well in advance of visiting the countries you are going to. Have all of your documents organized and ready to present in a quick, orderly fashion if you are going to places that have numerous check points.

Tip: Do something extra—clean up the beach, teach a local kid to surf.

Mail may be picked up at selected *American Express Travel Service* locations. The service is free for *American Express Card* holders, and travelers cheque customers. There is a small fee for others. To locate a *Travel Service* location, call (800) 528-4800.

MEDICAL CARE

Have any necessary **dental work** done well before your departure in order to avoid the pain that a change in cabin pressure can bring to new dental work.

Obtain a spare pair of **glasses** or **contacts** and a copy of your prescription.

Here's a weird one, but it works. **Ear cones** are a sort of hollow candle placed into the ear, which pull excessive wax and other unwanted debris from the ear. Check local health food stores and use only when necessary and as directed.

Pack prescriptions in clearly marked plastic prescription bottles. Keep your prescription with you, in case your luggage is delayed or lost. Pack over-the-counter drugs that may not be available during your travels. Pack convenient home-remedy instruments: thermometer (in a break-proof carrier), scissors, and tweezers, sunscreen and insect repellent.

Stingrays, those flat critters lurking in shallow, warm waters, can cause intense pain. The best way to avoid being hit by them is to shuffle your feet when you think that rays may be around. If you do get tagged and are a long way from a hospital, try putting your foot in hot water (as hot as you can stand it) for 45 minutes to an hour. Eventually you should have the wound checked by a doctor.

DISEASE INFORMATION

Good news comes from Linda Clarke at the office of *Travel Immunizations*. The vaccine, "Havrix" comes in a two-part series (six months apart) and protects against Hepatitis A. Havrix has been available in Europe for about 15 years, and those inoculated back then are still showing complete immunity to Hepatitis A, the virus transmitted by food and water. A very real concern for traveling surfers. For further information on immunizations, contact Linda Clarke at: Warren W. Pleskow, MD 317 N. El Camino Real, #406 Encinitas, CA 92024, (619) 436-3988. Thanks to the recently inoculated Gary Garside for this valuable tip.

Centers For Disease Control International Traveler's Hotline: (404) 332-4559.

MONEY

Traveler's checks, American dollars and major credit cards are good in most places. Write down all of the numbers of your cards, and keep them in a separate place. Don't carry a lot of money with you. Stash money well, and don't flash it around. Don't keep everything— money, credit cards, passport, etc. in one place. That way if you get robbed, you will have back-up. In an increasing number of countries, you will need to have a Personal Identification Number (PIN) to use credit cards. Check with your bank.

The fastest way to get money in a foreign country is *Western Union*: (800) 325-6000.

Tip: Don't carry more money than you plan on spending at one time.

Tip: Some *S&Ls* provide free travelers checks to customers.

Tip: Try to have about two days worth of foreign currency before you arrive at your destination. Hotels, restaurants and stores are not always good places to exchange currency. Try a reputable bank.

Tip: Signing up for the *"Express Cash Program"* through *American Express* entitles you to access funds at more than 87, 000 ATM locations around the world.

Tip: You are able to register all credit and ATM cards so that one phone call will cancel all you cards. Call (402) 392-2429.

THE LAW

Tip: If you can't avoid drugs, you might consider getting treatment. Don't travel with people who may be in possession of illegal drugs. In some countries, this can lead to a long imprisonment. Don't buy dope from people you don't know, or don't know very well. Marijuana may be plentiful in some cultures, but the local authorities make quite a bit of money busting you for it.

Tip: Know the laws. In some countries it is against the law for males to even walk the streets without a shirt on. In other places you could be arrested for spitting on the sidewalk. Just because you cross a border, doesn't mean that you can do whatever you want. The right to extend your arm ends at someone else's face. You're not at home. Remember, if you spray paint somebody's car, you might just get the cane.

HAZARDS

Sharks happen. In places like Northern California, South Africa, Australia, and to an increasing extent, Hawaii, shark attacks are becoming common against surfers. You might want to check with the locals before entering the water. If you see lots of sea life boiling near a rivermouth and there's nobody surfing, reconsider going out. If the surf is so good that you can't resist, try not to surf too early in the morning, or too late in the evening. Some won't be able to heed the warnings. To them, we say, "Good luck."

LODGING

Youth Hostels. They're not just for kids anymore, and now just about anyone can stay there. We strongly recommend those hostels endorsed by the *Youth Hostel Federation*. Many of their 5,000 hostels are located near prime surfing areas. Costs for a Youth Hostel card are: Adults: $25. Under 18: $10. Family: $35. Over 54: $15. Life member: $250.

Check out the *"Cabin Guide to Wilderness Lodging."* Virgin Islands, Mexico, California. Primitive-style cabins for about $14 per night. The *"Cabin Guide To Wilderness Lodging"* explains types of lodging available, and fees. Contact *Jet Setters Publications*, 5025 S. Eastern Ave., Ste. 358, Las Vegas, NV 89119

PHONES

When **dialing from another country**, you need to dial the International code (011) plus country code, plus area code, plus the phone number. You may need to omit "0" or "9" at the beginning of the area code. Phones in some countries may sound like the purring of the family cat on *Sudafed*. Don't expect the "ring" to sound exactly like the one you're used to hearing in your own country. Also, it might take a moment for the phone to begin ringing. Be patient.

Make sure you know what time it is where you are calling to. The long-distance operator (00) will tell you the time, or you can read about it in the front of the phone book. A basic rule is to add one hour for every 15 degrees of longitude. The further west you travel, the earlier it is; the further east you go, the later it is.

If you are staying in a hotel, find out how much they are charging you for calls before you dial out. Sometimes, especially in some European countries, you can pay a small fortune for phone calls in a hotel.

OTHER THINGS YOU MIGHT NEED

If you find yourself in Santa Barbara, check out *Magellan's* new outlet store. They'll give you practical demonstrations of the country's largest collection of travel accessories. The following sections contain some of the items available in the store and in their annual catalogue. The friendly, knowledgeable staff will answer any of your questions concerning the products that they carry. *Magellan's:* 1-800-962-4943.

- Leather Security Wallet - #SV601F - $16. 85
- Vinyl Security Wallet - #SV601V - $8.85

- Deluxe Money Belt - #SV605D - $11.85
- Neck Wallet - #SV603D - $11.85
- Leg Stash - #SV608 - $11.85
- Leather Currency Belt - #SV609L - $27.85
- Bra Stash - Money pouch attaches to bra. Go ahead and frisk me, big boy. #SV607 - $4.85
- Passport Cover - #SP621 - $12.85
- Anti-Pollution Mask - Filters out smoke, or the spraying used on some flights. #SP627 - $9.85
- Original Sea Bands - To control sea, air, and car sickness through acupressure. #IF376 - $9.85
- Ear Ease - Eases painful ear aches that some people experience in landing and taking off. Guaranteed! #IF378 - $9.85
- Berlitz Interpreter - Translates five languages -German, French, Italian, Spanish. 300 most commonly-used travel phrases and questions. #CL151 - $79.00
- World Mate Translator - #CL161 - $99.00 - 15 languages in the palm of your hand.
- Seiko Translators: Spanish - #CL154 - $29.85 French - #CL155 - $32. 85

Outlets and Electricity Your electrical gadgets might not work where you're taking them. Be sure to get the proper adapters or transformers.
- Adapter plug set.
  Adapter plugs for five of the most common plugs encountered in the world. #EA239F - $9.85
- Adapter plug A - #EA235A - $2.85
  Used in Western Hemisphere, North and Central Pacific. Adapts European plugs to American sockets, and polarized plugs to non-polarized sockets found throughout the world.
- Adapter plug B - #EA235B - $2.85
  Common in Great Britain, parts of Africa, Far and Middle East. Found in Great Britain and in its

former and present colonies.
- Adapter plug C - #EA235C - $3.85
  British Iles, some of Africa and China.
- Adapter plug D - #EA235D - $2.85
  The most common plug pattern around the world.
- Adapter plug E - #EA235E - $2.85
  South Pacific.
- Adapter plug F - #EA235F - $3.85
  Hong Kong, Indian subcontinent, some of Africa, former British colonies.
- Adapter plug H - #EA235H - $9.85
  South Africa and neighboring Namibia.
- No converter is needed if you plan to use dual-voltage appliances. Otherwise, you will need one to adapt between 110, 120, 220, and 240 volts. Some electrical items are not adaptable, so call *Magellan's* and be specific about where you're going, and what electrical appliances you hope to use overseas.

  You'll need one type of converter to use your heating - type appliances overseas (hair dryer, iron, etc.) and another for things like laptop computers. The "combination converter" handles both with the turn of a switch. Also protects your appliance from burning out if there's a problem with the wiring where you're staying. Considered a good value over individual converters.
- Combination Converter - #EA236A - $27.85
- Combination Converter Kit - #EA236K - $34.85
  Includes Combination Converter and the Adapter Plug Set.

First-Aid Kits
- International Travel Medical Kits
  Large - #KF503 - $49.50
  Regular - # KF403 - $29.50
- "Emergency Room" Trauma Kit for Travelers - #KF504 - $26.50

For medical/dental emergencies where there are no sterile needles and minor operating facilities available. Strictly for the hard-core.

- Dentanurse Dental First-Aid Kit - #KR525 - $19.85
  Temporary dental work kit in those countries where you don't trust anyone poking around your gums with the same knife they used to skin the iguana you had for dinner.
- Fabric Steamer - #EC213B - $28.85
  Takes the wrinkles out. Comes with 110-220 switch.
- Grundig YB 400 World Band Radio - #AR127 - $199

Bugs

- Hanging Mosquito Net - #SC506 - $64.50
- Permanone Repellent - #SC519 - $6.85
  Spray on clothing and bedding.
- "Skeeter Defeater" Tent - #SC503S - $49.50
- Double "Skeeter Defeater" - #SC503D - $59.50
  Weighs only one pound, but folds out into a cool mosquito tent. Fits over the bed if you like. Netting so small that even "no-see-ums" are denied entry.
- Bulk mosquito netting - #SC504 - $4.95/yd.

Tip: Avon Calling! From San Diego tube-monster Josh Tudor, comes this tip: "I've used everything to kill mosquitoes, and nothing worked that well until a friend loaned me a product called *"Skin So Soft,"* by *Avon.* The only place to get it is from the Avon lady, but it works better than anything I've ever tried, and I've tried everything." Surfer-pilot, and world traveler Doug Avazian, backed up Tudor's claim. Neither of these macho men, however, were able to explain what the Avon lady was doing at the door.

Cool, Clear Water

Many of the best places in the world have the worst **drinking water.** You have several choices: Drink beer, get a good portable water filter, a purifier, get sick. A filter treats water by screening out the bad stuff. The smaller the pores of the filter, the more stuff that you don't drink. A purifier disinfects the water usually with iodine or chlorine.

• PUR Portable purifier - #FH58IN - $49.
  Kills the things you wouldn't want to see under a microscope or crawling through your small intestine.

FOREIGN GOVERNMENT TOURIST OFFICES IN THE UNITED STATES

Australian Tourist Commission
1270 Avenue of the Americas
New York, NY 10020
(212) 489-7550
3550 Wilshire Boulevard
Los Angeles, CA 90010
(213) 380-6060

Bahamas Tourist Office
30 Rockefeller Plaza
New York, NY 10020
(212) 757-1611

Caribbean Tourism Association
20 E. 46th Street
New York, NY 10017
(212) 682-0435

French Government Tourist Office
610 Fifth Avenue
New York, NY 10020
(212) 757-1125
9401 Wilshire Boulevard
Beverly Hills, CA 90213
(213) 272-2661

Mexican Ministry of Tourism
630 Fifth Avenue
New York, NY 10020
(212) 265-4696
3106 Wilshire Boulevard
Los Angeles, CA 90010
(213) 385-6438

New Zealand Government Tourist Office
630 Fifth Avenue
New York, NY 10020
(212) 586-0060
10960 Wilshire Boulevard
Los Angeles, CA 90024
(310) 477-8241

FOREIGN EMBASSIES AND CONSU-
LATES IN THE UNITED STATES

Area code for all Washington phone numbers is (202).

Australia:
Office of the Embassy
160 Massachusetts Avenue, NW
Washington, D.C. 20036
Phone: 797-3000

Bahamas: (Commonwealth Of The)
Office of the Embassy
Suite 865
600 New Hampshire Avenue, NW
Washington, D.C. 20037
Phone: 338-3904

Barbados:
Office of the Embassy
2144 Wyoming Avenue, NW
Washington, D.C. 20008
Phone: 387-7374

Costa Rica:
Office of the Embassy
2112 S Street, NW
Washington, D.C. 20008
Phone: 234-2945

Fiji:
Office of the Embassy
Suite 520
1629 K Street, NW
Washington, D.C. 20008
Phone: 296-3928

France:
Office of the Embassy
2535 Belmont Road, NW
Washington, D.C. 20008
Phone: 234-0990

Mauritius:
Office of the Embassy
Suite 134
4301 Connecticut Avenue, NW
Washington, D.C. 20008
Phone: 244-1491

Mexico:
Office of the Embassy
2829 16th Street, NW
Washington, D.C. 20009

New Zealand Consulate:
1 Maritime Plaza Suite 700
San Francisco, CA 94111
Phone: (415) 399-1455

Women traveling alone need to be extremely cautious in some countries. In many places men will assume that a woman is loose if she goes into a bar alone, especially if she flirts with men she does not know. It is wise to observe how the local women act before venturing out on your own. If they are wearing veils over their faces, that should be a sign to at least cover your legs. Try to avoid drinking alone, or trying to change the local customs against women. You may find some of them deplorable, but remember that their traditions can go back about 2,000 years before you were born. In some places even harmless gestures like placing your arm on the back of a man's chair can be interpreted as a come-on. Don't go home with total strangers. If you want to keep conversation casual, don't hesitate to mention that you're married, whether you are or not. A convincing-looking wedding ring can be helpful.

There are absolute horror stories of women traveling alone in Third-World countries in order to find surf. I don't want to ruin the adventure that traveling alone can bring, but please be cautious.

The closest I ever came to seeing a woman raped occurred when I was traveling (alone) through New Zealand. I had met two attractive women from Auckland, and we drove from the small town of

Gisborne, into the country to find a pub. We found a quaint-looking place on the water, walked in and began playing pool. We were naively trading drinks with a band of about 10 men at the bar. As it got dark, it became evident that rape was on the mind of the all-male and, by now, very drunk bar patrons. There was nowhere to run, nobody else was around, and even the bartender was in on it. In a last ditch effort, we made a run for it. The car wouldn't start. I pushed while instructing my date in the subtleties of popping the clutch, as bottles and rocks and the beer-crazed mob got closer. We escaped, unharmed, but it taught me that even in a country known for it's hospitality, women need to be more cautious than men.

Big cities in almost any country in the world are usually rough places. It's far safer to be escorted by a man in those places than not. Sorry, ladies, that's just the way it is.

EMPLOYMENT

Most foreign countries require employment visas in order to work, but these laws are often casually enforced. To locate jobs legally, try the following addresses:

- International Executive Corps
  Box 10005, Stamford, CT 06904-2005
  Phone: (203) 967-6000
  Sends retired execs, and technical support
  personnel to various countries around the world.

- American Hotel and Motel Association
  1201 New York Avenue NW
  Washington, D.C. 20005
  Send an SASE to the organization if you are
  interested in finding overseas job opps.

CONVERSIONS

Temperatures: To convert Fahrenheit to Celsius, subtract 32 from the Fahrenheit number, multiply by 5 and divide by 9.

Kilometers are approximately 5/8 of a mile.

Liquids:

1 U.S. gallon = 3.79 liters

1 U.S. quart = .95 liters

6 U.S. gallons = 5 imperial gallons

Linear Measures, Customary:

one inch = 2.54 centimeters

one foot = 30. 48 centimeters

one yard = 0.91 meters

one mile = 1.61 kilometers

Linear Measures, Metric

one centimeter = 0.39 inches

one meter = 3.28 feet

one meter = 1.09 yards

SOME PHOTO TIPS

Get close to the subject, or get a longer lens. Think about it— how many travel photos do you have where the people look like nothing but colorful graffiti on a wall?

If you are really interested in the shot, use the best film and processing.

Get horizons straight.

Press the button, not the camera. Practice touching the shutter button with your finger only, and you will avoid some blur.

Buy a sturdy camera with a 35 MM lens. Some of the small automatic cameras are very good these days, and are convenient for travel. The *Weathermatic, Dual 35* by *Minolta* is inexpensive, waterproof and takes good photos.

If you are planning on sending some of the shots to a surf magazine, make sure that you are shooting slides, not prints. If it's a secret spot, keep it between yourself and a few friends.

P.S.: *Inclusion in " The Surfer's Travel Guide" is not necessarily an endorsement of the product or service mentioned. Make sure and check out all products and services in this or any other guidebook to the best of your ability. Be sure that restrictions on airline tickets don't hinder your travel plans.*

Bilderback-Courtesy Billabong

OAHU

FIRST GLIMPSE: *Surfer Magazine* or *Surfing Illustrated. Photos of Waimea, Sunset and Pipeline.*

First arriving in Hawaii in the mid '60s, I was about a decade too late to witness original tracks laid down at Waimea and Pipeline, but still early enough to ride some of the world's best waves with only a few people out. My luggage for the winter consisted of a Navy duffel bag with five T-shirts, three pairs of trunks, one pair of tennis shoes, four pairs of socks, a toothbrush, toothpaste, a bar of soap, a box of paraffin wax. All of this was wadded up in a nearly indistinguishable heap. My one and only surfboard, a Jacobs, Lance Carson Model, was taped up in my sleeping bag and hurled by attentive gorillas into the belly of the plane. My carry-on luggage was a sack soaked through from the grease of the fried chicken inside of it.

Not completely conscious of imitating Robert August and Mike Hynson, who were dressed in suits to board the plane in the original Endless Summer, I didn't realize how ridiculous I looked in sport coat and a wool turtleneck. The sweltering heat and the stares I received upon of my arrival caused me to ditch the jacket along with my wingtips in the Honolulu Airport bathroom trash can, where I changed into Levis and T-shirt soon after chugging an aquarium full of the free pineapple juice, courtesy of the Dole Pineapple Company, which used to have a dispenser there.

I stayed with my sister, who was living inland in Honolulu at the time, until I felt the urge to move on. Then I shifted to the water's edge, hoping to sleep on the beach at Waikiki. Naively, I had planned to camp out on the sand. I soon realized, however, that Honolulu was a big, modern city littered with skyscrapers, cars, cops, hookers, restaurants and pay toilets.

I was unrolling my sleeping bag as it got dark, and a very tall woman buried beneath a red wig staggered up the beach, golden spiked heels in one hand, martini in the other. She traversed the sands to discover my innocent, huddled frame curled beneath the balcony at Perry Boy's Smorgasbord. Having pity on me, she took my hand and walked me over the sand and up the street to her Cadillac. She stuck my board in the trunk. Within minutes we were zig-zagging out of Waikiki, beyond the hotels and tourists, beyond a row of strip bars on Hotel Street.

Somehow, the board avoided falling out of the trunk or getting any dings from being thrown around as she drove. She said her name was Genie (not her real name) and that she went by the stage name of "The Eye-Full Tower," when she worked as a stripper. She turned off the main street, up into a residential area. As we drove, she said that I could sleep on her couch if I wanted to.

"Are we near the beach?" I asked her.

"No," she said.

"Take me back to the beach, please." I requested politely.

She gave me a nasty look, flicked her cigarette half way across the street, threw a shaky U-turn, forced the bow of the Cadillac through traffic, flipping off cops and pedestrians before we ended up back in Waikiki. There, she pulled over to the curb and planted a long, wet kiss on me before I found myself dizzy on the street, in front of the Royal Hawaiian Hotel.

It was a full-moon night, and with three to four foot waves breaking out front of the hotel. I changed into my trunks and paddled out alone. Never before had I had such an experience, comfortably surfing crisp little curls to the light of the moon and tiki torches, faintly able to hear the sounds of the street in the background.

The waves were good, and I surfed until about 10 o'clock.. Then I came in, nearly dry from the warm, fragrant winds by the time I hit the beach, where I changed back into my Levis again. I spent that night where I had started, below the balcony of Perry Boys.

The next day I found a place to live in the "jungle" of Waikiki where I split $90-a-month rent on a dilapidated, one-bedroom house with four other surfers, a cute but wild runaway of 15 named Judy who we all tried, unsuccessfully, to look out for. We lived next to a couple of transvestites, who did our laundry once a week.

About a month later I transferred out to the North Shore, and moved into a place near Sunset Beach where the year before, a group of surfers led by Bill Andrews, lived rent-free in a condemned house, across from Kami's Market. They had no electricity, so they played Bob Dylan on an eight-track car stereo wired to a car battery that they left in the front room.

It was on the North Shore that I learned about respect, fear, and how to locate the keys to inward paradise. Almost daily, I watched Jock Sutherland, who was my age, surf alone all day long at Pipeline, losing his board just once and then casually bodysurfing in to retrieve it and paddle back out.

Not only Pipeline, but the entire North Shore was still relatively empty. Surfers were crammed into dark, moldy, ugly structures filled with broken wine bottles, torn, lice-infested mattresses, filthy kitchens and, if you were lucky, a rusty refrigerator. Just outside, however, the real world shone blue and bright. The nights passed quietly and star-filled. Work, if you could get any, paid nothing but I managed most of our rent when I took a part-time job with a traveling carnival for a while. Mostly, there was nothing to do all day but surf and wonder how you were going to come up with your share of the tab at the end of each month.

Pipeline, Waimea and Sunset, had all been conquered. The outer reefs were still only a dream. Brock Little was not yet born. Since there were no phone-in surf reports, you never knew if the waves were coming up or going down. Extremes in fear and joy were explored, as were all sorts of backyard cosmic consciousness experiments, many of which ended in disaster. There was no organized religion, but most everything seemed kind of holy, in a way.

It seemed that we lived on the edge of the world in those days, and sometimes a few of us would venture out to Pipeline on small days, grabbing rails, just like John Peck, or so we thought at the time.

For some reason, hollow rights were not surfed too often on the North Shore, and you could have all the Backdoor, Off The Wall, Rocky Point, then called Arma Hut, or Velzyland rights, alone, just about any time you wanted them. The North Shore was a world a million miles from the civilized world, a world with its own laws, and outlaws, where none but the fittest or the craziest survived. Girls were as rare as new towels. Nobody that I knew owned a TV.

I visited the North Shore again last year. All of the spots were crowded, and were surfed far better than when I was a kid. There was a big hotel complex where Jackie Baxter used to ride his motorcycle. It had all changed and more change was on the way. And yet, as I looked out, I could see that the ocean had not changed. In spite of cords, wetsuits, helmets, surf reports, crowds, and everything, the North Shore of Oahu still seems like the edge of the earth, a place a million miles from the civilized world.

BEST SEASON FOR SURF: Biggest waves usually occur on the North Shore between December and February. Often smaller, cleaner and less crowded a month or so before or after that. This is not a firm rule, however, big waves can arrive on the North Shore without much warning almost any time of year. Waves on the South Shore are generally best between late May to early October. From May through October, is the south swell season, where wave heights can reach eight to ten feet on South Shore beaches.

SURFBOARDS: If you plan surfing the North Shore in peak season, bring as many boards as you can afford to carry. You'll probably break some of them. Your hotdog board from home will work well on the small days. After that you'll need a good 7-foot plus board just to make the cut. If you plan on surfing Waimea or Sunset, get a board shaped by someone who has made plenty of North Shore boards. Try calling or contacting the following shapers: John Carper: (808) 682-4788, Eric Arakawa: (808) 682-4536 and Pat Rawson: (808) 638-8428.

Average charge for boards is $45 each way from West Coast of U.S. to Honolulu, or final Hawaiian destination. Make sure that you know the price before you book your ticket.

Tip: If you have two or more boards, try to pack them so that they look like one.

Tip: Take two extra strokes down the face when you ride Sunset.

Tip: Get a bigger board than you think you'll need if you plan on riding the North Shore for the first time.

Tip: If you are going to Hawaii after the season has

ended, you might be able to buy a board from one of the visiting pros who is selling off some of his quiver. Try to get a board from someone who is about your weight. There are often good used boards for sale at some of the surf shops on the North Shore. Don't expect to rent or borrow a really good big-wave board. For one thing, they break.

Tip: Try to get a board that will show up well in a rip. Greens and blues can be easily lost in a rip.

OTHER SURF ACCESSORIES: Rashguard, and maybe a vest for early mornings, late evenings. At least two very heavy leashes, and a lighter one.

Tip: For the novice, keep in mind that the surfer first up and closest to the breaking part of the wave, has the right-of-way.

Crowds are a factor almost everywhere on Oahu. Still, there are a lot of waves, and on some days it can seem uncrowded.

AIR TRANSPORTATION: Because it is one of the most frequently flown routes in the world, the flight between Honolulu and Los Angeles is one of the best values per-flight-miles in the world. While the standard fare is a bargain, there are ways to save yet more money. The flight takes about 4 1/2 to 5 hours from the West Coast of the U.S.

     Air charters can be money savers, but call the *Better Business Bureau* and local or *State Consumer Protection Bureau* to find out whether complaints have been lodged against the company you plan on flying with. Pay with credit card if you can, and consider trip-cancellation and default insurance.

Tip: Check around for those coupon books sold by local charities. A good one is called *"Entertainment '95"* (updated yearly) in which there are discount coupons on both *Continental* and *American Airlines*. There are also discounts on restaurants, rental cars, and hotel accommodations, with some hotels offering a 50 per cent discount to coupon holders. As with all discounted airfares, there are probably some limitations on when you can travel. *Entertainment Publications, Inc.* can be reached at: P.O. Box 7067, Troy, MI 48007-7067.

DOCUMENTS: A U.S. Citizen does not need a visa or a passport to travel to Hawaii, and can move there much as they would from any other region of the country. If you plan on traveling beyond Hawaii, it is advisable to get an International Driver's License. For those coming to Hawaii from outside of the United States, an International License is essential in order to drive legally. In the U.S., an International Drivers License can be obtained from AAA for $10. It is good for one year. There is no test, but you will need to show a valid driver's license, plus two passport-sized photos. Out-of-state drivers need to have their licenses renewed before expiration date. Those coming from other countries, check with travel agent or appropriate embassies for visa and passport requirements.

GROUND TRANSPORTATION:
Shipping a car to Hawaii costs about $800 each way. Call *Matson* at: (800)-4-*MATSON*, or *Auto Freight Link*: (619) 336-1070.

Cars in Hawaii require a safety sticker. If you are buying a car, make sure that the sticker has some time left on it. If not, be sure that the car will pass inspection. Shop the local newspapers for used cars, or check around at the local youth hostels.

Car Rentals

If you are renting your car in a package deal with your flight, the *Hawaii State Consumer Protection Office* suggests that you ask whether the company will honor a reservation rate if only larger cars are available upon your arrival. Find out which credit cards are accepted.

Cars are around $35-$45 per day at the airport and about $5 less per day in Waikiki, with lower rates available at local budget companies. Most companies offer unlimited mileage. *Dollar* has a good daily value. *Budget* has a good weekly rate. During peak seasons (summer, Christmas vacation and February) car rentals require reservations.

A mainland driver's license is valid in Hawaii for 90 days. A Hawaiian driver's license can be obtained for $8.50 at the *Honolulu Department of Motor Vehicles* at 1370 Maunakea Street: (808) 532-7700.

Alamo: (800) 327-9633
Avis: (800) 831-9633
Budget: (800) 527-7000 - Ask about the **free** certificates to Hawaii's top attractions.
Dollar: (800) 367-7006
Hertz: (800) 654-3011
Aloha Funway Rentals: (808) 831-2277 (a good place for convertibles and Jeeps)
Five-O: (808) 836-1028
VIP (808) 732-3327
United: (800) 922-4605
Maxi Car Rental: (808) 923-7381

You may not need to purchase insurance on your rental. You may be covered by your own policy. Check with your insurance agent before entering Hawaii. If you are covered, bring along a photocopy of the benefits section of your policy.

If you are interested in surfing only the Waikiki

area, there are at least 35 breaks within walking distance from any point.

Biking the North Shore

If you are interested in surfing only the North Shore area, a bicycle and a board rack like the *Wheele*, are portable, and can get you and your board around nicely, especially with the Ke Ala Pupukea Bike Path which will run from the northern end of Ho'alua Street near Sunset Beach to Three Tables, giving good access to 3.5 miles of prime surfing lands.

Buying a car

If you intend on staying in Hawaii more than a month, the best thing is to buy a car. Cars on Oahu are more expensive than they are on the U.S. mainland. The rusting of a car is only the most apparent problem. Check the car out thoroughly, and make sure that it has some time left on the safety sticker. You can score a good deal on a car if you find someone ready to leave Oahu. Bulletin boards at supermarkets and anyplace where backpackers hang out, are good places to find cheap cars. *The Honolulu Star Bulletin*, or any one of the daily community newspapers are also good places to check. Check with other surfers, but keep in mind that someone who is planning on buying and selling a car quickly is not likely to have taken very good care of it.

Buses: If you need transportation to a beach, catch the bus which services most of the beach parks. Call 531-1611 for routes and schedules. Surfboards and other large gear are not allowed on city buses.

LODGING:
Home Search Network: (808) 623-9195
P.O. Box 3133, Miliania, Oahu 96789

Tip: Check out the *Hawaii Vacation and Relocation Directory:* $2.00

If you are staying on the South Shore, there are numerous good hotels that vary in quality and price. If you are traveling in peak season, and want to stay near the water, it is best to get a reservation.

Youth Hostels, Backpackers etc.
Write to *American Youth Hostels:*
733 15th Street, NW, Suite 840, Washington D.C. 20005, USA. Phone: (202) 783-6161. American Youth Hostels are open to people of all ages, and a YHA card entitles you to entrance to approximately 5,000 youth hostels worldwide. Credit Card Bookings in the USA: (202) 783 6161.
All Hawaii numbers are (808) area code.

Back Packers: 638-7838
Hawaii Seaside Hostel: 942-3306
Hawaii Style Hostel: 949-3382
International Club Hostel ,Waikiki: 926-8313
Kim and Don's: 942-8748
Poly: 922-1340
Shower Tree: 839-1386
Waikiki Prince: 922-1544
Honolulu—University: 946-0591
Sunset Beach Realty: 638-6300
Bed and Breakfast Honolulu: (800) 288-4666

Camping
State parks are open year-round. There are no entrance, parking, picnicking or camping fees. Permits can be obtained at most any district office of the *Division of State Parks.* District Office: P.O. Box 621, Honolulu, HI 96809. Phone: (808) 587-0300. Street address: 1151 Punchbowl St.

- Kahana Valley State Park
  52-222 Kamehameha Highway (Highway 83),
  Kahana.
- Keaiwa Heiau State Recreation Area
  Inland a bit, but a nice place to visit.
- Malaekahana State Recreation Area
  Call 293-1736 for lodging and camping.

State Park Lodging: Housekeeping cabins, and
single-unit cabins accommodate a maximum of six persons each. Rates: one person, $10, two persons: $7, on
down to $6.50.

City and County of Honolulu Beach Parks (parks
are not limited to Honolulu area):

- Bellows Beach Park
  41-043 Kalanianaole Highway
  Waimanalo
- Hau'ula Beach Park
  54-135 Kamehameha Highway
  Waimanalo
- Kahe Point Beach Park
  92-301 Farrington Highway
  Ewa Beach
- Kaiaka Recreation Area
  66-449 Haleiwa Road,
  Haleiwa
- Kea'au Beach Park
  83-431 Farrington Highway
  Waianae
- Kualoa Regional Park
  49-479 Kamehameha Highway
  Kaneohe
- Lualualei Beach Park
  86-221 Farrington Highway
  Waianae

- Mokule'ia Beach Park
  68-919 Kaena Point Road
  Waialua
- Nanakuli Beach Park
  89-269 Farrington Highway
  Nanakuli
- Swanzy Beach Park
  51-369 Kamehameha Highway
  Kaawa
- Waimanalo Bay
  Recreation Area
  41-043 Aloiloi Street
  Waimanalo
- Waimanalo Beach Park
  41-741 Kalanianaloe Highway
  Waimanalo

Permits are free and may be obtained from the *Department of Parks and Recreation* in the Honolulu Municipal Building (HMB) at 650 South King St., ground floor, or at any satellite City Hall.

For more information call *The Permit Section*: (808) 523-4525.

Other camp sites
- Camp Timberline: (808) 671-2239
- Camp Mokuliea Episcopalian Church:
  (808) 637-624

FOOD: A lot of good roadside food. Plate lunches are a good deal. Good fruit available in most markets. Main market on the North Shore: *Foodland*, on Kam Highway, across from the fire station. This is also a good place to communicate, find cheap cars and speculate on coming swells. Every famous surfer you've ever seen will show up there at one time or another. Convenience stores: *Kami's Market* and *Sunset Market,* both near

Sunset Beach. Food is expensive, and a *Cost Co. Card* from the mainland can save you money. For Honolulu *Cost Co.*, call 422-7140. For Hawaii Kai, call: (808) 396-5546.

A free Hawaiian Visitor's Card can be obtained by calling 1-800-GO-HAWAII at least 30 days before your departure date. The card entitles you to savings of up to 55 percent on long-distance calls from Hawaii. They will also provide you with an 800 number to use.

PETS: Unless you plan on staying in Hawaii for a long time, it's a good idea to leave Fido at home. Because there are no rabies in Hawaii, there is a long quarantine on dogs.

MEDICAL CARE:
All Hawaiian phone numbers are (808) area code.
Hospitals:
Castle Medical Center: 263-5500
Kaiser-Permanent Moanalua Medical Center: 834-5333
Kapiolani Medical Center for Women and Children: 973-8511
Queen's Medical Center: 538-9011
Straub Clinic & Hospital: 522-4000
Doctors on call:
Hyatt Regency Waikiki: 923-1234
Outrigger Waikiki: 971-6000
Kuhio Walk-In Medical Clinic: 924-6688
Queen's Medical Healthcare Center: 943-1111
Ala Moana Hotel, Pacific Beach Hotel: 926-7776
The Honolulu Physicians' Exchange: 524-2575
Hawaii Dental Association Hotline: 536-2135

Some Important phone numbers:
Hawaiian Visitors Bureau: 923-1811
Information and Complaint: 523-4385

Honolulu International Airport: 836-6413
Office of Consumer Protection: 586-2630
Better Business Bureau: 942-2355
Bishop Museum: 847-3511
ASK-2000 (Information and referral service): 275-2000.
Weather and Ocean Information: Recorded National
Weather Service forecasts: 836-0121.
Marine Forecast: 836-3921
Surf Report: 836-1952

NATURAL HAZARDS:
- The Portuguese Man-of-War:
  Victims should be carefully observed for symptoms
  of feeling ill, shock, severe pain, swelling, dizzi-
  ness, fainting, unconsciousness, cramps, breathing
  difficulties, convulsions, heart problems, and
  vomiting. Follow up with a visit to a doctor.
- Coral cuts are prone to infection and are slow to
  heal in tropical temperatures. Staph is a major concern. Cuts should be cleaned thoroughly and checked
  periodically for infection.

For detailed information, obtain a copy of *Dangerous Marine Organisms* by Athline Clark. Write to
UH Shea Grant Publications, 1000 Pope Rd., MSB 200,
Honolulu, HI 96822.

UNNATURAL HAZARDS: Some of the surfers on
Oahu can be heavy. Give respect, and don't take off on
them, and you'll have a better time.

Q: How does a haole speak pidgin in Hawaii?
A: Don't!

Tip: Try to avoid bringing anything that says "Team"
on it. Believe me, nobody will be impressed by anything but good surfing.

Tip: If the surf is over 6 foot, watch a few sets, see where people paddle out, and get in. Time the sets, and watch for boils on the face, indicating shallow areas. If you are lucky enough to be in a position where there is nobody out, watch for longer than you normally would. What looks like a big, mushy peak from shore, could turn out to be a very dangerous reef.

Tip: Okay, you're a haole. You can't hide the fact, but you don't have to advertise it either. Sweatshirts that say "Iowa State" or "California Fox" might not go over too well with the locals. Keep the camera in the bag until you check the vibe.

Tip: Practice swimming and paddling, and get in the best shape of your life if you plan on surfing the North Shore. This goes for other regions where the surf has the potential to drown you.

Tip: Waimea, real Waimea, which the locals claim doesn't happen until the waves top 18 feet (Hawaiian standard, which means a 6-foot wave is about double overhead) is not the big, mushy peak that it appears to be from shore. If you are going out there for the first time, check it from all angles. The hill on the Haleiwa side of the bay will show you how hollow the place can be.

Tip: Try to adjust to the standard that everyone else uses for calling wave height. In Hawaii it is common for waves to be measured from the back rather than the face. Don't argue about it, it's a time-honored system. Therefore, a double-overhead wave will most likely be called "6 feet." And remember, a 6-foot wave in Hawaii probably packs more than twice the volume of water, moves faster, and is breaking on a shallower reef than wherever you came from.

Tip: Where to buy that special muumuu.
Oops, wrong book.

SURF SHOP GUIDE
Honolulu:
Blue Hawaii Surf Inc.
1960 Kapiolani # 108, (808) 947-5115
New surfboards, bodyboards, accessories, clothing, and ding repair.

Classic Surfboards
(808) 842-4761
Manufactures surfboards, and repairs dings.

Downing Hawaii
3021 Waalae Ave., (808) 737-9696
Sells and rents surfboards, bodyboards, surfing accessories, clothing, ding repair.

Hawaiian Island Creations
Ala Moana Shopping Center, (808) 941-4491
Sells surfboards, bodyboards, surf accessories, clothing, ding repair.

Local Motion
1714 Kapiolani Blvd., (808) 955-7873
Sells and rents surfboards, bodyboards, accessories, clothing, ding repair.

Hawaiian Island Creations
King's Alley, (808) 971-6715
New, used, custom surfboards, bodyboards, surfing accessories, clothing.

Town & Country Surf Shop
Waikiki Trade Center, (808) 923-9998
Sells surfboards, bodyboards, accessories, clothing.

Local Motion
Koko Marina Shopping Ctr., (808) 396-7873
Sells and rents surfboards, bodyboards, accessories,
clothing, ding repair.

Russ K. Makaha
1500 Kapiolani Blvd. Suite # 101-B
Honolulu, HI 96814, (808) 951- RUSS

North Shore
Barnfield's Raging Isle Sports
66-250 Kam Hwy. , (808) 637-7707. Sells and rents
surfboards, bodyboards, surf accessories, clothes, repair service. Makes custom surfboards.

Strong Current
66-250 Kam. Hwy., (808-637-3406)

Sunset Beach Surf Shop
59-176 A Kam Hwy., (808) 638-7097
Sells surfboards, bodyboards, accessories, T-shirts, ding
repair.

Xcel Wetsuits Hawaii
66-4700 Kam Hwy., (808) 637-6239
Sells surfboards, bodyboards, surf accessories, clothing, ding repairs.

*If you would like your Hawaiian surf shop listed
in the next edition of* The Surfer's Travel Guide, *be sure
and write to us, and we'll include your listing, free of
charge.*

NON-SURF THINGS WORTH SEEING: Bishop
Museum, Commsat, Waimea Falls, Kaena Point.

Q: How to get to the Kodak Hula Show.
A: And you call yourself a surfer.

A free copy of the *Digest of Fishing Laws and Rules* can be obtained from the *Hawaii Division of Aquatic Resources,* Kalanimoku Bldg., Rm. 330, 1151 Punchbowl St., Honolulu, HI 96813. Phone: (808) 548-4001. For enforcement information or to report a violation, call the *Conservation Hotline*: (808) 548-5918.

A complete guide of dive spots can be obtained for $2.00 by writing the University of Hawaii, Sergeant Extension, MSB, 1000 Pope Road., Honolulu, HI 96822.

FURTHER ON: Oahu is truly the gateway to the Pacific, a home-base for those who want to explore a world of surf. It will also prepare you for reef waves that you will encounter in the South Pacific. Check the *Honolulu Star Bulletin* Sunday paper "travel section" for cheap flights to places like Tahiti, Fiji, Australia and New Zealand. Also, the outer islands. Check the "Air Transportation" entry under the "General Information" section of this book.

"Everything else — California, Australia and South Africa is off Broadway –The North Shore is Broadway."

— Terry Fitzgerald

Cassidy

MAUI

FIRST GLIMPSE: *Surfer Magazine. Later, some promotional stills for the movie "Free and Easy," featuring shots of Honolua Bay with Herbie Fletcher and Bill Fury. I didn't get up close and personal with Maui until 1969. Man, it was big, and man, Les Potts was the man. We camped in a tent on military property, and wondered why nobody was surfing the outside reefs at Sprecklesville. Saw the biggest surf of my life at Hookipa Park—the same waves that hit the North Shore and threw houses across the street on Kam Highway, made Honolua Bay perfect. Rainbow Bridge, baby.*

BEST SEASON FOR SURF: November-February. The biggest surf on Maui's north shore is often plagued by onshore winds. Not suprisingly, many of the best surfers on the island are also good windsurfers. Maui has fewer, but better quality breaks than almost any of the other islands in the Hawaiian chain. Honolua Bay, considered one of the best right points in the world, and the magical but inconsistent Maalaea illustrate the point. Two of the most consistent spots on the island, Hookipa Park and Lahaina Breakwall, keep a large group wet when nothing else will. When Maui goes flat in the summer, it can be absolutely fl-lat—nothing, not a wave, not a ripple.

Summer surf
Summer is not really a great time to be a surfer on Maui. What surf there is, usually happens mostly around Lahaina. Can be good, but never much over 4 or 5 feet. Keep coral cuts clean. Staph can be a real problem. If you get lucky, Maalaea might break while you're there. One of the stand-by places that nearly always has surf

67

is Hookipa Park. A passable summer spot with waves more often than not, for those who have to surf, and don't mind dodging windsurfers.

SURFBOARDS: The surf on Maui is generally cleaner than that of the North Shore, and you can ride a somewhat smaller board. A longboard is a good idea for those nearly flat days that often happen. If you plan on surfing "Jaws," I guess you could ride a 7'6", but you will also need a wave runner, a boat and foot straps.

If you booked your flight from the U.S. mainland, the cost of the board being sent inter -island should be covered to your final destination. If you booked a flight from the Honolulu Airport to Maui, expect to pay $20 per board, each way. Try to wrap your boards so that two or more look like one. Read "Packing your board" in the "General Information" section of this book.

OTHER SURF ACCESSORIES: The offshore winds in the mornings and evenings can be cool. A vest will do. Bring a rashguard. Extra leash. Tropical wax.

WEATHER AND CLOTHING: Mostly warm days and nights. Bring light, casual clothing. Rain can be expected in winter, but not much around Lahaina, which is the dry side of the island. If you plan on visiting the Haleakala Crater, bring a warm jacket. The crater is located at 10,000 feet and it gets cold enough to snow there.

National Weather Service, Maui Forecast: (808) 877-5111.

CROWDS: Because there are so few spots of quality, and half the North Shore flies there every time that it closes out (a good indication that Honolua is good) the main breaks on Maui can be extremely crowded.

AIR TRANSPORTATION: Kahului Airport: (808) 872-3800 is the only airport on Maui that offers direct service from the U.S. mainland. *United Airlines:* (800) 241-6522 flies direct from Los Angeles, Chicago, San Francisco. *American Airlines*: (800) 433-7300 also flies into Kahului Airport but makes a stop in Honolulu from Los Angeles, Chicago, Detroit, Houston, St. Louis, New York and Dallas. *Delta:* (800) 221-1212 has service direct to Maui from Los Angeles, Atlanta, Dallas, and Salt Lake City. If you plan on spending time on Oahu before visiting Maui, you can book with your travel agent to fly there from the Honolulu Airport.

Add at least one hour of flight time if you are connecting to Maui from Honolulu. Flights from Honolulu: *Continental:* (800) 525-0280, *Hawaiian:* (800) 367-5320, *Northwest:* (800) 225-2525, *TWA:* (800) 221-2000. Flights to Maui from Honolulu take 20 to 30 minutes. Price is about $50, one way, and flights are available many times daily on *Hawaiian Airlines, Aloha:* (800) 367-5250 and *Mahalo Airlines:* (808) 833-5555. Flights usually run from about 6:30 a.m. through 8 p.m.

GROUND TRANSPORTATION: Unless you are being picked up at the airport, it is wise to book a car in advance and pick it up at the airport. Kahului is near some good winter surf, but you probably won't be staying on that side of the island. Most major car rental companies have conveniently located desks at each airport. During peak seasons—summer, Christmas, Easter, have a car reserved. Bring a set of soft racks if you want to get a small economy car. Expect to pay about $35 for a compact car.

If you are planning on staying in Maui more than a month, it might be a good idea to buy a cheap car. The local paper, the bulletin boards at the backpackers spots, and at Maui Community College are good places to check into buying cars. If you are getting a "Maui cruiser" expect rust, and ripped upholstery. Do, however, check out the running condition of the car, and be sure that it will pass a safety inspection. Make sure that there is quite a bit of time left on the safety sticker.

There used to a be a saying on Maui concerning old cars, "If it makes it to the Bay, it's okay." The laws are not as slack as they used to be, but if you are planning on staying more than a month on Maui, it still might be a good idea to buy a car. Cars are considerably more expensive than on Oahu.

CAR RENTALS: The majors are all well represented in the larger towns and at the airport. One of the local car rental agencies might provide a better deal.

Word of Mouth Rent a Used Car: (800) 533-5929
Wheels R Us Lahaina: (808) 667-7752
VIP: (800) 367-6080
Quick Tips: (808) 244-8934
AA Paradise Network: (800) 942-2242
Cars R Us: (808) 572-2722
LTAR. As low as $200 per month, cash or credit cards: (808) 874-4800.
Payless: (800) 729-5377
Cost Less: (808) 833-0030
Discount: (808) 941-0658
Tradewinds: (808) 834-1465
Paradise Jeeps: (808) 946-7777

ROAD SERVICE: One AAA garage offers 24-hour island-wide service: *Sunset Towing:* (808) 667-7048.

LODGING: Over the decades, much of Maui has given way to mega condos and resort development. As well as being ugly, these places are expensive. There are still some cheap places to stay, however. Try Banana Bungalow: (808) 244-5090

SunTrips offers a variety of excellent packages, including lodging, rental cars and combinations of islands. 2350 Paragon Dr., San Jose, CA 95131. Phone (408) 432-0700.

Mana Kai-Maui
Walea/Kehei
From $100, includes car, breakfast and hotel room (Prices subject to change.)
(800) 237-9851

Camping:
District Office
54 South High Street
Wailuku, HI 96793
(808) 243-5354

Polipoli Spring State Park
At 6,200 feet in the Kula Forest Reserve. About 10 miles upland from Kula on Waipoli Road off Kekaulike Ave. (Hwy. 377). Four-wheel drive recommended. Camping and lodging, one cabin. Far from the surf, but beautiful forest area and views of Central and West Maui, Kaooawe, Molokai and Lanai. Pig and seasonal bird hunting, if you're into it. Don't be fooled, just because you're in Hawaii. You're at 6,200 feet, and nights get cold, and can drop below freezing in winter. No showers.

Waianapanapa State Park
At the end of Waianapanapa Road off Hana Hwy. (Hwy 360). More than 50 winding miles east of Kahului Airport. It takes about three hours. Remote, wild, low-cliffed volcanic coastline. Solitude is the best single word to describe it. Lodging, camping, picnicking, shore fishing, hiking. Small beach. Waves not far away within season. Worth the trip.

Fees are charged for cabins, but not for camping. Obtain permits from district office. Permits issued from 8 a.m. to 4 p.m. Monday through Friday, except holidays. Permits can be obtained by persons 18 or older. Permit applications must be received at least seven days in advance of use, and no earlier than one year in advance. Priority for camping and lodging permits will be issued in order of: 1) Walk-in applicants, 2) Mail-in applicants, 3) Phone-in applicants.

FOOD: The two major supermarkets open 24 hours on Maui, are: *Safeway* Hanopiilani Hwy., *Safeway* 170 E. Kamehameha Ave. Try *Farmer's Market* in Kahana. Excellent produce at a fair price, in the parking lot of the *ABC Store* at 3511 Lower Honopiilani Hwy. Open Monday 12:30 p.m.-4:30 p.m., Thursday 9 a.m.-noon. Kahului *Foodland,* 1881 S. Kihei Rd. Kihei.

MEDICAL CARE
Hana Medical Center: Hana Hwy., Hana: (808) 248-8294.
Kula Hospital 204 Kula Hwy., Kula: (808) 878-1221.
Maui Memorial Hospital, 221 Mahalini, Wailuku: (808) 244-9056.
Doctors on call: (808) 667-7676 Maui Physicians, 3600 Lower Honopilani Rd., Lahaina: (808) 669-9600. West Maui Healthcare Center 2435 Kaanapali Pkwy., Suite H-7, Kaanapali: (808) 667-9721. Kihei Clinic and Wailea Medical Services 1993 S. Kihei Rd., Kihei (808) 879-1440.

Pharmacies *Long's Drug Stores*, Kahului: (808) 877-0068. *Kihei Drug*, Kihei Town Center: (808) 879-1915.

SOME IMPORTANT PHONE NUMBERS
Office of Consumer Protection: (808) 243-5387
Hawaii Visitor's Bureau, Maui Chapter: (808) 871-8691

Kahului Airport: (808) 872-3803 or 872-3893
Hana Airport: (808) 248-8208

Maui Swap Meet: Everything from someone else's junk to authenic Hawaiian antiques. Located at the Kahului Fairgrounds Hwy. 35 Sat 8-1. $3 per car.

SURF SHOP GUIDE
Da-Kine Hawaii
W. Kuiaha Rd.: (808) 575-2495
Surfboards and accessories.

Hi Tech
444 Hana Hwy.: (808) 877-2111
New and used surfboards, sailboards, bodyboards, rentals, ding repairs, accessories, clothing.

Hobie Sports
845 Front Street, Lahaina: (808) 661-8848
Lahaina Cannery Mall: (808) 661-5777
2411 S. Kihei Rd.: (808) 874-0999
New and used surfboards, bodyboards, accessories, clothing.

Hunt Hawaii
120 Hana Hwy.: (808) 579-8129
New,used and custom surfboards and sailboards. Rentals, ding repairs, accessories, clothing.

Lightning Bolt, Maui Inc.
55 Kaahumanu, Suite E (808) 877-3484

Local Motion
1819 S. Kihei Rd., Kihei: (808) 879-7873
1295 Front Street, Lahaina: (808) 661-7873
Rents and sells surfboards and bodyboards, accessories, clothing, ding repairs.

Maui Surfing School
(808) 877-8811
Surfing lessons. Also sells and rents surfboards and bodyboards.

Ole Surfboards
1035 Limahan Pl., Lahaina
(808) 661-3459
Sells and rents surfboards and accessories. (Ole is one of the finest surfboard makers in the Islands.)

NATURAL HAZARDS: Watch coral cuts which can easily become staph infected and turn to serious wounds.

UNNATURAL HAZARDS: Some of the locals and especially the transplants can be a little rough at times.

NON-SURF THINGS WORTH SEEING: Visit Haleakala Crater, Seven Sacred Pools, Hana, Iao Valley.

KAUAI

FIRST GLIMPSE: Mark Martinson at a place called "Whispering Sands." The waves were nice and small, the way we liked them then. Kauai seems to have acquired all of the breaks that were due to Maui.

Stories of Kauai's "Taylor Camp" still circulate, as do tales of Joey Cabell at big Hanalei Bay. The great Pacific drop-out zone has not been the same since "Fantasy Island." There are crowds and restaurants, and an increasing number of tourists. Still, there's nothing like a major hurricane to let you know that you are right on the edge of the Pacific Ocean. Kauai is still a prime destination filled with lots of real Hawaii. The locals don't ask for respect for themselves or their island. They demand it.

BEST SEASON FOR SURF: Between November and February for the north shore breaks. South shore breaks generally work best between late May and early October.

SURFBOARDS: Everything from a longboard to a fairly substantial gun. Mostly bring a board that will handle fast, hollow reefs in the 6-foot range. What would you ride at Rocky Point? Bring that. If you have arranged for a ticket from the U.S. mainland, you should be able to have your board sent for no extra charge to your final Hawaiian destination. If you are booking an inter-island flight, expect to pay $20 per board, one way. If you have more than one board in the bag, try to make it look like there is only one.

OTHER SURF ACCESSORIES: Some prefer booties and thin wetsuits for shallow reefs. Bring an extra cord. Tropical wax. Rashguard. Vests are nice for mornings and evenings.

WEATHER AND CLOTHING: Go neat, casual and light. Bring something for rain and some sort of rubber sandals for your feet.

CROWDS: Can be crowded at the main breaks.

AIR TRANSPORTATION: *United Airlines* discontinued its direct flight service from the mainland to Lihue Airport after Hurricane Iniki smashed into the island a few years back. Check with the airlines for an update, as there is some talk that direct flights from San Francisco may start up again.

Carriers to Lihue include: Mostly from Oahu, *Aloha Airlines:* (800) 367-5250. *Hawaiian Airlines:* (800) 367-5320 and *Mahalo Airlines:* (808) 833-5555. Expect to pay about $75 each way. Boards are about $20 each, one way, unless you have booked them through to your final destination. It's a 25-minute flight, leaving several times daily from Honolulu.

Cheap Flights: Check the "General Information" section, under the "Air Transportation" entry in this book.

GROUND TRANSPORTATION: From the airport by bus: Since Iniki, Kauai has decided to have the communal last laugh, by establishing the "*Iniki Express.*" (808) 241-6410. The bus ride is free.

Car rentals
Daily prices start at $35. A fly/drive deal can sometimes reduce the rate a little. Remember to take your

soft racks so that you can get everything into a compact. There is a $2 per day surcharge on all rentals.

Car rental facilities near the airport are:
Alamo: (800) 327-9633
Avis (800) 831-8000
Budget: (800) 527-0700
Dollar: (800) 800-4000
Hertz: (800) 654-3011

Cheaper car rentals
There are some deals available on used rental cars. Check around, or try: *Westside U-drive:* (808) 332-8644. Rentals start at $19-95 and Jeeps start at $59. 95. Cars are well maintained and the company offers free delivery and pick-up of your vehicle at your hotel or condo.

Buying a car
If you plan on staying more than a month, it's not a bad idea to buy a car. Expect to pay quite a bit more than you would on Oahu, and make sure that the car has a safety sticker or meets safety requirements.

LODGING: Not a lot of dirt-cheap lodging in Kauai. But fear not, we're going to steer you into rooms under $60 a night. Sorry, boss, that's the best we could do.

- Hale Lihe Motel: Clean rooms in a nice location. Ask about air conditioning. 2931 Kalena St., Lihue 96766. Phone: (808) 245-3151. Credit cards not accepted.
- Hotel Coral Reef: Clean, older hotel. 1516 Kuhio Highway, Kapaa 96746. Phone: (808) 822-4481. On the beach, near good surf.
- Kauai Sands: Same area, similar price. Good place for the money. Air- conditioned. Kitchenette avail-

able for a few more bucks. 420 Papalaloa Rd., Kapaa, 96746.
- Garden Isle Cottages: Good place with phones and TV. 22666 Puuholo Rd., Koloa 96756. Phone: (808) 742-1681.
- Kay Baker's Bed & Breakfast: They say that just meeting Kay is reason enough. Aloha spirit meets country soul. P.O. Box 740, Kapaa, 96746. Phone: (808) 822-3073. No credit cards. Phone: (808) 822-4951.

Camping
Kauai District Office
3060 Eiwa Street
Room 306, Lihue, HI 96766-1875
(808) 241-3444

Kauai County Parks and Recreation Department
444 Rice St., Room 230
Lihue, Kauai 96766
(808) 245-1881

- Kokee State Park: Located 15 miles north of Kekaha on Kokee Road (Hwy. 550) at 3,600 feet; adjoins Waimea Canyon State Park. No surf.
- Polihale State Park: Location at the end of 5- mile dirt road from Mana Village, off Kaumualii Hwy. Wild coastline with large sand beach backed by dunes. Camping is free. Cabins are $10 for first person, and drop from there for additional people.

MEDICAL CARE:
Doctors Kauai Medical Group (KMG): Main clinic located at 3420-B Kuhio Hwy, Lihue 96766: (808) 245-1500.
Other KMG facilities are located in Kilauea: (808) 828-1418. Princeville: (808) 826-6300, Kukui Grove: (808)

246-0051, Koloa: (808) 742-1621, Kapaa: (808) 822-3431. Mon., Thurs., Fri. 10: 30 a.m.-1:30 p.m.; Sat. Noon-6 p.m.; Sun. 10 a.m.-4 p.m. Doctors are on call 24 hours. Call: (808) 245-1813 after hours.

Hospitals:
Wilcox Memorial Hospital 3420 Kuhio Hwy., Lihue 96776: (808) 245-1100.
Kauai Veterans Memorial Hospital 4643 Waimea Canyon Dr., Waimea 96796: (808) 338-9431.

Pharmacies:
Long's Drugs in Lihue. Kukui Grove Center Hwy. 50: (808) 245-7771.
Kapaa: *Shoreview Pharmacy*, 41177 Kuhio Hwy., Suite 113: (808) 822-1447.
Haapepe. *Westside Pharmacy* 1-3845 Kaumaualii Hwy.: (808) 335-5324.

SURF SHOP GUIDE
Hanalei Surf Company
5-5161 Kuhio Hwy.: (808) 826-9000. Sells and rents surfboards and bodyboards. Surf accessories, clothing, lessons.

Poipu Surf & Sport
Kiahuna Shopping Village: (808) 742-1132
New and used surfboards, bodyboards, rentals, ding repairs, accessories, clothing.

Wailua Surf Shop
4356 Kuhio Hwy.: (808) 822-3035
Sells and rents surfboards, bodyboards, accessories, clothing, ding repairs.

If you have a surf shop and would like to be included in this section, please send the appropriate information to us, and we'll include you in our next printing, free of charge.

NATURAL HAZARDS: Reefs, and occasional and increasing shark attacks.

UNNATURAL HAZARDS: Heavy locals and transplants can throw a vibe in some places.

FURTHER ON: There are other islands in the Hawaiian Island chain that can be approached from Kauai. Surf explorers will be rewarded if they look hard enough. The best deals on international flights will generally be through Honolulu.

Captain Cook landed on Kauai on Jan. 20, 1778. In two centuries since Hawaiian colonization, most of the Hawaiian population has been wiped out, and at least 23 species of animals have become extinct and another 30 are in danger. The ocean remains beautiful, but there is still some resentment. Modern explorers, tred lightly.

Dible

CALIFORNIA

FIRST GLIMPSE: Rincon, 1962. Dawn, eight-to-ten feet, perfect.

First glimpse: Malibu, 1962. Mid-day in July. Four-to-five feet with 100 surfers out. Mickey Dora and Lance Carson dominating.

Surfing didn't begin in California, but much of the surf culture and the attitudes of our sport have its roots here. With the movie industry being a large part of the surf scene, it's no wonder that the Golden State has become the land of the poser. Only in a place like this could you be a surfer without getting wet. But, make no mistake, some of the most hard-core surfers in the world live and surf here. And while a growing population continues to threaten our existence, there are still a number of user-friendly pockets on this 1,000 miles of coastline, places that, when conditions are right, make this one of the best places on earth to surf.

The surf is pretty accessible in Southern California, mostly right off the highway. North of Santa Cruz, the surf is a little more elusive, cold, and rugged. If you are not sure of where to find it, pull into one of the hundreds of surf shops that dot the coast, and ask. Conditions vary from decent beach breaks to classic points, to out-of-control, you could lose your life out there, cloudbreaks. For the seeker, there are still some excellent spots to be found.

One of the big advantages of traveling in California is that surfboards and associated accessories are readily available and relatively inexpensive. New boards cost $300 on up at the surf shops, and are even less expensive when going through the manufacturer, most of whom are listed in the local yellow pages, or in *this guide. Wetsuits, leashes, rashguards, board bags, and clothing are a far better deal here than in most other surf locations, so stock up before you head any further.*

BEST SEASON FOR SURF: November through February. But good surf can occur at any time.

SURFBOARDS: A basic mid-six thruster will cover most of your needs. A longboard is a good thing to have. Guns are only needed on rare occasions, but are an absolute necessity if you plan on Mavericks or Todos, which is just below the Southern California border. California is the land where anything goes, and you'll sometimes find bodyboards, longboards, and tiny twin-fins sharing the same break. Waves are generally gentle and easy to ride in Southern California. In Northern California, the surf is usually much larger and challenging.

OTHER SURF ACCESSORIES: Between November and February, a fullsuit is needed even for Southern California. Booties are often used north of Santa Barbara. Other seasons can be handled in a spring suit. On the warmest days, you won't need anything but a bathing suit and a rashguard. The water rarely gets above 70 F. A great concentration of competent to excellent board makers work in California. Getting a board from one of them might be a good idea.

CROWDS: Yes. It can get very crowded especially in mid summer (July-August). Lots of kooks this time of year, but at least most kooks are friendly.

AIR TRANSPORATION:
Arrival: Mostly by air at *Los Angeles International Airport.*

Cheap Fares: Since it's a primary destination, there are numerous good deals to and from Los Angeles, San Francisco or San Diego. Shop the Sunday newspaper. Check under "Air Transportation" in the "General Information" section of this book.

GROUND TRANSPORATION: A car is nearly a necessity in California, and since there are so many of them in Southern California, a decent one can be yours for a lot less than you might imagine. Large, luxury cars from the mid to late '70s are generally a very good deal. Chevys, Fords, Oldsmobiles all tend to run a long time, are easy to work on, but not so good on gas. A decent car of this vintage can easily be found for about $1,000 and sometimes as cheaply as $500. Station wagons are about as versatile as vans, but since they lack the youth appeal of vans, they can be purchased for a lot less money. A good, American-made station wagon has the potential to last a long time, is good to sleep in, is a powerful workhorse, and can carry you, a few friends, surfboards and all your gear. Expect to pay anywhere from $1,000 to about $1,500 for a decent American-made station wagon built in the mid to late '70s.

Depending, of course, on the condition of the vehicle purchased, one of the aforementioned cars could easily get you around this great state. It's a good idea to buy a tool set, however, just in case. For those raised on *Starsky and Hutch* and *Night Rider*, Good News! All but bowling alley lounge lizards and urban cowboys loathe Trans Ams. They can be purchased for very little money in California. Just don't expect women, except those with bouffant hairdos, pink poodles, and *Road Runner* T-shirts, to come flocking.

Have the engine, transmission, tires etc., checked and be aware that most U.S. cars require a smog certification at transfer. If the car you desire is polluting the atmosphere, you will not only suffer guilt over the matter, but you could be restricted from driving it.

Its a good idea to get a AAA card, which offers good road service, maps, and limited free towing. They can also insure you. Liability insurance is the minimum requirement and covers you should you smack your inexpensive pile of tin into someone's very expensive pile of tin.

Public transportation sucks here, but private transportation is doing just fine. The place was designed for cars, lots and lots of them.

All the major rent-a-cars are at the airport. Taxis and buses will take you to the main parts of town and to hotels. Certain parts of Los Angeles can be dangerous. Try to stay far away from downtown.

USEFUL WORDS AND PHRASES: "Have a nice day." Learn to draw out the word "day."

PETROL or what we Americans call gas, is about $1.25 a gallon. Convience stores and off-brand stations are least expensive.

LODGING: Youth Hostels are surprisingly sparse in California, especially Southern California. Camping in Southern California is also sparse, and it is not advisable to try to sleep on public beaches. There are however, numerous inexpensive motels throughout the state, *Motel Six, Budget Motel,* and some off-brand roadside places offer clean rooms from about $30 a night and up. At more expensive hotels, good deals can be had through coupon books. Sometimes the kindness of strangers will be pressed upon a particularly well-mannered foreigner.

Youth Hostels:
Youth Hostel Credit Card Booking Number: 0202 783 6161.

San Diego
- Point Loma
  Hostelling International
  Elliott Hostel, 3790 Udall St.
  San Diego, CA 92107-2414
  Phone: (619) 223-4778, $12
  Reservations suggested
- Imperial Beach
  Phone: (619) 239-2644
  Nice beaches, good waves, hideous pollution.
- San Clemente Youth Hostel
  Phone: (714) 492-2848

Los Angeles
- Los Angeles International Youth Hostel. 1502 Palos Verdes Dr., North Harbor City (213) 831-8109. Former Navy barracks near Long Beach harbor. (Not a pretty area, but a port in a storm). Accessible by bus from *L.A. International Airport*. Around $10 per night.

San Pedro
- Hostelling International
  Los Angeles, South Bay, 3601 South Gaffey St., Building 613, San Pedro, CA 90731
  Phone: (310) 831-8109
  Fax: (310) 831-4635, $11.50

This is not a hostel, but when the going gets weird... Worth a look. Some surf in area.
- Venice Beach Hotel
  1515 Pacific Avenue

Venice, CA   90291
(310) 452-3052, $75 a week
- Hollywood YMCA and Youth Hostel, 1553 N. Hudson Ave., Hollywood, CA (213) 467-4161 Single rooms start at about $20. Blankets available. Hostel rates start at $10 for members or non-members. Pool and gym available to all.
- Mary Andrews Clark Home YWCA
306 Loma Dr., Los Angeles, CA
There was no listing when we called the phone number. Reports are that this is a cool refurbished mansion with room for 138 women (and 138 men desperate to gain entrance). Breakfast and dinner in cluded in rate of about $30 for YWCA members. $35 for others. *Master Card* and*Visa* accepted.

Central Coast
- Hostelling International
Point Montara Lighthouse
P.O. Box 737, 16th St. at Cabrillo Highway 1
Montara, CA 94037
Phone: (415) 728-7177, $9-.$11.
- Monterey Hostel
P.O. Box 1013, Monterey, CA 93942
Phone: (408) 649-0375, $6
- Pescadero (Near Mavericks)
Hostelling International
Pigeon Point Lighthouse, Pescadero CA 94060
Phone: (415) 879-0633, $9.-$11.
Reservations suggested for Friday/Saturday
- Hostelling International
San Luis Obispo
SLO Coast Hostel, 1292 Foothill Blvd.
San Luis Obispo, CA 93405
Phone: (805) 544-4678, $ 13.
Reservations suggested.

- Santa Cruz
  Hostelling International
  315 Main St.
  Santa Cruz, CA 95061
  Phone: (408) 423-8304, $12-$14.

San Francisco
- Hostelling International
  Building 240, Fort Mason
  San Francisco, CA 94123
  Phone: (415) 771-7277, $13.-$15.
  Reservations suggested
- The Embarcadero SF YMCA
  166 The Embarcadero at Mission Street
  (415) 392-2191
- The Central YMCA
  220 Golden Gate Ave.
  (415) 885-0460. About $30.
- YWCA Hotel
  620 Sutter Street
  (415) 775-6500.
  Women only.

Northern California
- Point Reyes National Seashore
  Hostelling International
  Point Reyes Box 247, Point Reyes
  Station, CA 94956
  Phone: (415) 663-8811, $9.-$11.
  Reservations suggested
- Redwood National Park
  Hostelling International
  14480 Highway 101 at Wilson Creek Road
  Klamath, CA 95548. $9.-$11.
  Reservations suggested.

CAMPING: Many of the State Parks are adjacent to good surf, and while the State Park system is a good one, offering convenience and comfort to the camper, camping is not that cheap. Sites begin at $18 per night. From June through September, there is a long waiting list. A good alternative to camping might be one of the numerous inexpensive motels along the coast.

To make reservations for State Parks call *MISTIX* at (800) 444-PARK. *VISA, American Express*, or *Maser Card* are accepted. From outside the continental U.S. call (619) 452-1950. Hearing impaired, call *MISTIX TDD* (800) 274-7275.

CAMP SITES:

- **Andrew Molera State Park**

In the Big Sur area. A must-see area for the first-timer to California, this stretch of coast features some of the most spectacular views and trail walks you'll ever see. There is good surf in the region, but it is highly prized by the protective locals. Tread lightly.

- **Del Norte Coast Redwoods State Park**

Beautiful area, great beaches. Weather often wet and foggy. Some good surf in area.

- **Prairie Creek Redwoods State Park**

A great place to stop and see the elk, and walk in the redwoods. Some surf in the area. Weather often wet and foggy.

- **Humboldt Lagoons State Park**

Typical beautiful beach setting. Often plagued by wet fog. Some surf in the area.

- **Patrick's Point State Park**

A stunning place to camp. Often plagued by wet fog.

- **Westport-Union Landing State Beach**

Classic north coast. Beautiful beaches, rugged coastline. Some surf in the area.

- **MacKerricher State Park**

Similar to Westport-Union.

- **Russian Gulch State Park**

As with most of the north coast, this is a beautiful, sometimes foggy area.

- **Van Damme State Park**

Classic north coast beauty.

- **Manchester State Park**

Similar to Van Damme. Some good surf in the area.

- **Sonoma Coast State Park**

The wine country. Classic California. Some surf in the area.

- **Half Moon Bay State Beach**

A wet area, and a place of massive north swells. Mavericks is no secret anymore. Be cautious if you plan on surfing the area in the winter—December-February. Big gun territory. Warm wetsuit. Fake smile. Go.

- **New Brighton State Beach**

Santa Cruz is a surf town. Lots of good surf in town itself, and beyond that there are some great little coves and secluded beaches. Surf all year round, but mostly in the winter. Visit one of the many local surf shops and they'll clue you in.

- **Sea Cliff State Beach**

Similar to New Brighton

- **Sunset State Beach**

Similar to Sea Cliff State Beach.

- **San Simeon State Beach**

Imagine that all the tourists are gone, and you can get a glimpse of old California. Some surf in the area.

- **Morro Strand State Beach**

Windy, cold, foggy. Other than that, a nice place. Some surf in the area.

- **Morro Bay State Park**

Similar to Morro Strand State Beach.

- **Montana De Oro State Park**

Be prepared for the wind. Some good surf in the area.

- **Pismo State Beach**

This is right about where the north coast unofficially begins. The more adventurous among you will want to keep heading north. Decent beach breaks at times.

- **Gaviota State Park**

A decent camping area, important because it is the gateway to the Hollister Ranch, and some of California's best, and most protected surf. The Ranch itself is private. Numerous schemes abound to try and gain access. Most are denied.

- **Refugio State Beach**

A nice spot, not far enough from the dismal realities of Los Angeles. Rarely surfed, but it is reported to be good on occasion.

- **El Capitan State Beach**

A nice place to camp. Certain seasons bring good waves.

- **Emma Wood State Beach**

Camping a little too close to town for most. Recreational surf at times.

- **McGrath State Beach**

Some fertile wave grounds near by.

- **Leo Carrillo State Beach**

A nice place, especially considering it's so close to L.A. Decent little waves. Often crowded. Watch which colors you wave.

- **Doheney State Beach**

Once a classic place. Then came the harbor, and unbelievable pollution. Doheney and especially Dana Point are *the* examples of what happens when apathy hits town. Killer Dana is dead.

- **San Clemente State Beach**

Good camping, decent surf. Not far from the classic and consistent points of Trestles. Be prepared to walk.

- **San Onofre State Beach**

Summer camping only. Near San Onofre State Beach, where good longboard waves, surf history and good times abound. The West Coast's answer to Waikiki, without all of those dumb hotels, of course. Try to ignore the nuclear power plant.

- **South Carlsbad State Beach**

Decent surf in an area that was once a quiet pocket, but has been discovered by the land vultures.

- **San Elijo State Beach**

A nice place to visit. Good beach. Good waves break on the reefs. Slow, and not very consistent in summer.

FOOD: Everything you ever wanted to eat and then some. Supermarkets are well stocked with everything. Small, Mexican food take-outs are a great deal. 7-11 is a good place to get quick, cheap food, gas, magazines and the new hit game "Rump Shot."

WATER: Water is drinkable from the tap throughout California. A better source of water for health and taste's sake, however, is one of the many bottled waters available in nearly all stores.

PHONES: City Codes: San Diego: 619. Los Angeles: 213 & 310.
Emergency: Phone: 911
Information: Phone: 411

MEDICAL CARE: Some of the best hospitals in the world, and good medical care exist in just about every town, regardless of size. Pharmacies are common and well stocked, and you can get most any prescription filled at *"Thrifty"* or *"Long's" drug stores*. There are good hospitals and *"Redi Care"* units in most medium sized and big cities. Good insurance is helpful. There are no unusual health problems.

HIV: Take normal precautions.

SOME SURF SHOPS:

O'Neill Surf Shop
1149 41st Ave.
Capitola, CA 95010
(408) 475-4151
Rentals, repairs, surf reports, O'Neill Wetsuits & accessories.

Infinity Surf
24382 Del Prado
Dana Point, CA 92629
(714) 661-6699
Full service—repairs

Hansen Surfboards
1105 First Street
Encinitas, CA 92024
(619) 753-6595

Encinitas Surfboards
107 N. Highway 101
Encinitas, CA 92024
(619) 753-0506

Rusty Surfboards
201 15th St.
Del Mar, CA
(619) 259-3200

Sunset Surfboards
897 First Street
Highway 101
Encinitas, CA 92024
(619) 753-7229

Hobie Oceanside
1909 South Hill Street
Oceanside, CA
(619) 433-4020

The Longboard Grotto
987 N. Highway 101
Encinitas, CA 92024
(619) 634-1920
Full Service-specializing in used longboards (Over 200).
Huge memorabilia section.

San Onofre Surf Shop
3305 S. El Camino Real
San Clemente, CA 92672
(714) 366-6660

Rip Curl
3801 South El Camino Real
San Clemente, CA 92672
(714) 498-4920

Becker's Surf Shop
301 Pier Avenue
Hermosa Beach, CA 90254
(310) 372-6554
(310) 456-7155 - Malibu
(714) 364-2665 - Mission Viejo

Harbour Surfboards
329 Main Street
Seal Beach, CA 90740
(310) 430-5614

Bruce Jones
16927 Pacific Coast Highway
Box 269, Sunset Beach, CA 90742
(714) 840-6500

Just Longboards
904-916 Aviation Blvd.
Hermosa Beach, CA 90254
(310) 376-8847
Full service and repairs

Wind an Sea
127 Main Street
Huntington Beach, CA 92648
(714) 374-0160
Three locations. Full service

The Frog House
6908 West Pacific Coast Highway
Newport Beach, CA 92663
(714) 642-5960

Kanvas By Katin
16240 Pacific Coast Highway
Newport Beach, CA 92663
(310) 592-2052

Freeline Design
821 41st Avenue
Santa Cruz, CA 95062
(408) 476-2950

South Coast Wind n'Sea
740 Felspart Street
Pacific Beach, CA 92109
(619) 483-7660

South Coast Longboards
5037 Newport Avenue
San Diego, CA 92107
Tel (619) 223-8808
Fax (619) 223-9215

The Green Room
1963 Abbott Street
San Diego, CA 92107
(619) 226-1311

Harry's Surf Shop
705 Felspar
San Diego, CA 92109
(619) 270-3886
Full service
Home port for Skip and Donna Frye and Hank Warner

Pancho's Surf Shop
187 Pomeroy
Pismo Beach, CA 92449
(805) 773-7100
Full service and repairs

Sundance Ocean Sports
2026 Cliff Dr.
Santa Barbara, CA 93109
(805) 966-2474
Rents surfboards, bodyboards, wetsuits

Channel Islands
29 State St.
Santa Barbara, CA 93101
(805) 966-7213

Full Bore Surf Shop
12925 El Camino Real
Del mar, CA 92130\
(619) 792-7019

Hang Ten Surfboards 1321 Calle Valle, Suite P
San Clemente, CA 92672
(714) 366-9411

Stewart Sports
2102 S. El Camino Real
San Clemente, CA 92672
(714) 492-1085
Full service—300 board inventory

Star Surfing Co.
4655 Mission Blvd.
San Diego, CA 92109
(619) 273-7827

RD Surfboards
17221 E. 17th Street
Santa Ana, CA 92701
(714) 558-3775

Bob's Mission Beach
4320 Mission Blvd.
San Diego, CA 92109
(619) 483-8837

Mitch's Surf Shop Supply Central
631 Pearl
La Jolla, CA 92037
(619) 459-5933

SeaSide Surf Shop
2571 South Highway 101
Cardiff by the Sea, CA 92007
(619) 753-6649

BJ's
111 W. Plaza
Solana Beach, CA 92075
(619) 792-8823

Toes On The Nose
903 S. Coast Hwy.
Laguna Beach, CA 92651
Phone/Fax: (714) 497-3292

Pearson Arrow Surfboards
2320 Mission
Santa Cruz, CA 95060
(408) 423-8268
Capitola (408) 475-8960
Full Service

Santa Cruzn'
723 Soquel Ave.
Santa Cruz, CA 95062
Large collection of longboards.
(408) 458-5360

Waveline Ventura
154 E. Thomas Blvd.
Ventura, CA 93001
(805) 652-2201
New and used longboards. Accessories, repairs, surf
reports.

Coral Reef Dive & Surf
7041 14th St.
Westminster, CA 92881
(714) 894-3483
Full service. Custom Wetsuits

Witt's Carlsbad Pipelines
2975 Carlsbad Blvd.,
Carlsbad, CA
(619) 729-4423

SURFBOARD MANUFACTURERS:

Bain Surfboards: (619) 753-0255
Byrne Surfboards: (619) 721-6094
Channel Islands Surfboards: (805) 966-7213
Channin Surfboards: (619) 753-7989
Dynamic Balance: (619) 632-6613
Eaton Surfboards: (619) 224-5603
Eberly Surf Designs: (619) 943-8045
Goodrum Surfboards: (619) 599-9295
Hawaiian Freestyle: (619) 755-6629
Hawaiian Pro Designs: (619) 967-9790
Linden Surfboards: (619) 722-8956
Moonlight Glassing Company: (619) 942-3319
Rusty Surfboards: (619) 578-0414
Skip Frye Surfboards: (619) 270-3886
Sauritch (619) 436-0345
Van Zanten: (619) 793-1057
West Coast Laminating: (619) 743-4099
Weber: (619) 259-1084
Xanadu: (619) 678-0468

Sorry if we missed you. If you would like your surf shop or board building services included in The Surfer's Travel Guide, *and it fits into one of the mentioned regions, please let us know, and we will be glad to include you, free of charge in our next printing.*

NATURAL HAZARDS: Most everything dangerous, except for some drive-by specialists, are either illegal, dead or in a cage.

UNNATURAL HAZARDS: Driving in rush-hour traffic, smog, theft and possible violence in population centers. A few of the surf spots are highly localized. Watch for signs of pollution after a hard rain.

FURTHER ON: There are lots of good deals on air travel in Southern California. A good shopper will find deals to Hawaii, Australia, all over the South Pacific, Mexico, Europe, Central and South America. Driving to Mexico, Central or South America is pretty direct, but not without it's hazards. Check the "General Information" entry under "Air Transportation."

McNabb

BAJA

FIRST GLIMPSE: *1965. Waking up on the side of the road at a place called "Stacks" near Ensenada to four to five foot surf with nobody out. We had driven in the night in a $100 Ford station wagon (rest its soul) which eventually ended up dying south of the border.*

BEST SEASON FOR SURF: Good surf can be had along the Baja Peninsula at any time, but November-February and the month of September can often have the biggest surf.

SURFBOARDS: For the points, any type of hotdog board from a wide noserider to a small thruster. If you're thinking of going out to Todos Santos Island on a big swell, better make sure not to under-gun.

OTHER SURF ACCESSORIES: It's deceiving. Usually the further south you go in the northern hemisphere, the warmer it gets. But right near the U.S./Mexican border is where the water begins to get cold, sometimes as much as 10 degrees colder than in Southern California. It stays that way nearly to Cabo San Lucas. Blame it on the Kioshiro Current. Full wetsuits, even booties, are needed in winter. A fullsuit is not out of the question even in summer, but usually a spring suit will suffice. Bring at least one extra leash. Bring a range of surf wax, from "tropical" for Cabo, to "cool," for everything else. Bring a ding-repair kit. Bring everything you need when you travel for surf, because there are few places to buy surf accessories down there.

WEATHER: 1-900-WEATHER

CROWDS: Only at the main breaks.

AIR TRANSPORTATION: There are flights available to some of the more remote points, Islé Natividad, and Cabo. For cheap flights, check the "travel section" of a major newspaper, or see the "Air Transpiration" entry under the "General Information" section of this book.

DOCUMENTS: U.S. citizens are required to have proof of citizenship and a tourist card. This can be a valid U.S. Passport and a birth certificate or a certified copy, a voter's registration card, a notarized affidavit of citizenship or military discharge papers. A driver's license is not enough.

Tourist Card: All persons who plan to visit the interior of Mexico are required to obtain a tourist card or *Tarjeta de turista*. They are not necessary for anyplace north of Ensenada, and they are rarely asked for even in the deeper regions of the peninsula.

Check with your travel agent for latest requirements. Tourist cards are available with proof of citizenship at Mexican Government tourist offices or the Mexican Consulate, through some travel agents and, sometimes, through AAA.

Citizens of countries other than the U.S. and Canada should obtain an entry document at the nearest Mexican Consulate. Resident aliens in the U.S. are advised to check with U.S. Immigration prior to departure to Mexico. This will help to avoid problems upon re-entry to the U.S.

Mexican Consulate Offices:
Los Angeles: Consul General, 2401 West 6th St., 90057. Phone: (213) 351-6800.

San Diego: Consul General, 610 "A" St., Suite 100, 92101. Phone: (619) 231-8414.
Miami, Florida: Consul General de Mexico, 780 N. W. Le Jeuene Rd., Suite 525, 33126. Phone: (305) 441-6780.
New York: Consul Honorario, 1875 Harlem Rd., 19423. Phone: (716) 895-9800.

GROUND TRANSPORTATION: Mostly by car. A good, sturdy four-wheel drive. No sissy-mobiles (you won't need chrome on the differential or an airbrush of Cindy Crawford on the door). Other cars make it also, and some of the favorites among the locals include those big American cars from the '70s. The locals can fix them (or just about anything else) with a roll of bailing wire and duct tape. Avoid air-cooled Volkswagen Vans. They look nice, but they overheat and die. The road is littered with their carcasses. A U.S. driver's license is valid in Mexico.

During heavy seasonal rains (January-March), road conditions can become difficult and travelers can become stranded. For road conditions between Ensenada and El Rosario, Mexico, travelers can contact the nearest Mexican Consulate, tourism office or the U.S. Consulate General in Tijuana.

Driving under the influence of alcohol, possession of firearms, or carrying any illegal drugs, can lead to major complications in any part of Mexico. The fines for possession or distribution of marijuana can be extremely stiff. The jails aren't nice.

Insurance: Driving in Mexico without insurance is a felony. If you are in an accident (regardless of whose fault it is) you will be detained until an insurance adjuster can determine who was at fault. This usually takes a few hours.

Call your insurance company for quotes on insurance, and make sure that you know exactly what is covered. Also, there are large billboards on the San Diego/Mexican border which advertise Mexican insurance by the day.

For those who plan to visit Mexico often, an annual Mexican automobile premium can be expensive. *Oscar Padilla Mexican Insurance* now offers an annual policy where you only pay for the number of days you intend spending in Mexico during the year. The insured can select a policy anywhere from 15 to 180 days a year. Contact *Oscar Padilla Mexican Insurance,* 1660 Hotel Circle N., Ste. 735, San Diego, CA 92108. Phone: (619) 688-1776 Fax: (619) 688-1948.

Tip: Hide a few $20 bills in your car, just in case the federales take all of the money in your wallet.

Tip: Watch the signs carefully. If the federales pull you over things can usually be settled on the roadside for $20. If they ask you to follow them to the station, do it.

Tip: Don't sleep in your vehicle along the roadside at night.

Legal Assistance: *A.S.S.E.T. Defense Legal Mexicana,* S.A. de C.V. offers judical assistance and legal defense to drivers who have been in an accident in Mexico. Phone: (011) 52 83 44-04-48 or 44-04-50 or 43-42-04. You might want to keep this number in your wallet, just in case.

Highway signs: *Speed limits are in kilometers*
No Passing: *No rebase*
Use right lane: *Conserve Su Derecha*
Inspection: *Inspecion*
Keep Right: *Circulacion*

Tip: If you get a flat in the sand and your jack won't hold, put rocks beneath the car's axle, dig out, and change the tire.

Baja is the longest peninsula in the world. 1,300 kilometers of points, bays, reefs, and beach breaks.

Stay alert. Make sure that your car is in peak condition, and that you are prepared to fix it if it breaks down. Bring spare parts and lots of water, not only for drinking, but for a possible leaky radiator.

When filling up, make sure that the gas pump is at zero and that you are charged the correct amount. The octane numbers on the pumps can be misleading. *Magna sin*, the higher octane of the gas at the pumps, has a U.S. octane rating of 87, which is the rating for regular-unleaded in the U.S. *Magna sin* is found in the green pumps. *Nova* is in the blue pumps. We suggest that you go for the green in most cases. An octane booster is not a bad idea either.

The test comes when you hit the open road. There are long stretches here, with nothing to do but play your favorite tapes, sleep, eat, or read if you're lucky enough to be in a passenger seat. Get good instructions, and take advantage of any gas stations that you see along the way.

Make sure and drive carefully, as large, fast tractor-trailers regularly make their way down the narrow highway. Also, keep a close eye out for livestock, which can wander onto the road, kill the animal, anger the locals, and ruin your car. Many seasoned Baja travelers are leary of driving at night in Baja. The long expanses of highway between spots can prove hypnotic.

Central Baja is sparse, clean, and open. This is where some of the best points on the peninsula can be found, but they are hard-won secrets that people are quite protective of.

Miscellaneous: Bring a good tool box, an extra spare tire, extra fan belts, a good first-aid kit, a good knife, good flashlights, matches, firewood, water, canned and fresh food, surf wax, 5-gallon container of gas and everything you are going to need to go surfing. There are no surf shops or 7-11's down here, so make sure that you have everything you are going to need for your journey. Some of the good surf spots also feature good beach fishing or diving. Leave a copy of your itinerary at home with somebody. Check with a U.S. passport agency to see if travel advisories are in effect.

LANGUAGE: Spanish, but passable to excellent English is spoken near the population centers.

CURRENCY EXCHANGE: One U.S. dollar = 5.54 pesos. *Exchange rates will fluctuate.*

ELECTRICAL CURRENT: 110 V, 60 cycles, AC

Tip: Don't pick up hitchhikers, or go to Mexico with people that you don't know very well. Once we picked up a guy, only to find out that he who was running heroin from Tijuana to La Paz. He told us horror stories of the jails he had been in, and his torture at the hands of the federales. We dropped him off at the nearest cactus. Twenty minutes later, we were being searched by the federales. If that guy had been with us, we would still be in Baja.

LODGING: If you plan on spending the night in northern Baja, there are many hotels which range from decent to excellent. With all of the development in recent years, camping has become difficult to find. There are numerous private, gated communities where the surf is good, and where, for about $90 a day, you can have a clean house complete with a T.V., usually a VCR, an ocean view, and all the comforts of home. One of the best of these is Los Gaviotas, just a few miles south of Rosarito Beach. There is a good point break at the complex. It works best in the winter, but also picks up summer swells. And there are good beach breaks and points to the north and south of Gaviotas.

The following amounts are in pesos, and the rate of exchange can vary. Rest assured, it's a lot cheaper than it looks. A Youth Travel Plan Card can provide a wide range of discounts in Mexico. Cards are available from Agencia Nacinla de Turismo Juvenile, Glorieta Metro Insurgentes Local CC-11, Col. Juarez, Mexico DF CP 06600. Phone: 525 26-99, 525-29-74, 525-21-53.

Hostels etc:
Cabo San Lucas, Baja California Sur
Phone: 30148
Reservations: One month in advance.
$20,000 pesos

La Paz
Villa Deportiva Juvenilen
Blvd Forjadores 3km, Carretera al Sur
La Paz BCS CP 23040
Phone: 24615
Reservations: 15 days in advance
$20,000 pesos

Tijuana (I guess everybody has to check it out once in a lifetime, but good luck.)
Tijuana, via Oriente y Puente Cuauhtemoc s/n,
Tijuana BC, CP 22320
Phone: 47510, 49504
$20,000 pesos

CREA Youth Hostel
Avenida Padre Kino
U.S. $ 4.50

Campgrounds:
Camping is available at most of the major points for free, or at a slight fee. Please be sure to keep the area clean, burn toilet paper, and completely extinguish any fires you start. While there was once good camping in northern Baja, it is now almost entirely the domain of the overly-sterile and completely soulless R.V park.

San Miguel De Allende, Gto.
Phone: (465) 2-23-01
Cost: US $9 for two. Additional person: $2

San Miguel
Trailer Park La Siesta
Phone: (465) 2-02-07
Cost: US $9 for two. Additional person: $2

La Paz, B.C.S.
Phone: (52) 682-2-3761
Cost: US $13 for two. Additional persons: $1

Other places to stay:
Hotel Casablanca
Phone: (684) 3-03-30
Cost: US $ 8

FOOD: There is a variety of good food throughout Baja. Bread and canned foods are available in the markets. Mostly good Mexican food at the restaurants. Be sure that food is thoroughly cooked. Avoid raw vegetables in restaurants. Wash and peel any fruit that you buy in Mexico.

I once entered a Mexican restaurant with a British friend of mine. He took one look at the menu and asked; "They eat mole here?" "It's pronounced Moe-lay " I said to his relief.

Much of the food in Mexico is a bit spicy for those not used to it.

More than a dozen years ago , my friend Ralph Torres, and I were traveling in Baja when we stopped to buy some small rolled tacos, known as carnitas, at a little roadside stand. We inhaled the first dozen, which were delicious. We ordered a dozen more for the road. The man behind the counter smiled, and pulled a pig's head from a shelf below him. The fuzzy ears, the countless flies, the watery, unforgiving eyes which stared at us, all contributed to a change of mind as he began to carve meat from the poor animal We left without picking up our order. The point is, you need to be careful in Baja, especially with chicken, pork, or raw fish. Also, make sure that you drink bottled water, canned or bottled drinks.

Tipping: Standard is 10 to 20 per cent in restaurants. Bellboys, hotel maids, attendants, car watchers.

Water: Bring a good supply of water. Bottled water is available in the towns. If not, resort to beer or soft drinks in cans or bottles.

PHONES: Country Code: (52). City Codes: Tijuana (66). Cabo San Lucas (114). La Paz (112).

MEDICAL CARE: Adequate medical care can be found in cities. Care in remote areas is limited or non-existent. Additional health information is available from the Center for Disease Control's International Traveler's hotline at (404) 332-4559.

Disease Information: A certificate of vaccination against yellow fever is required for persons over six-months old, coming from infected areas. Ironically, yellow fever vaccine is not recommended for persons under nine-months.

Recommended Immunizations: Update tetanus/diphtheria, measles/mumps/rubella, and polio vaccines as appropriate to age and date of last dose, and Havrix (which is covered in "General Information") for Hepatitis A. Typhoid vaccine is recommended for travelers visiting areas other than major resorts who are anticipating extended stays. Hepatitis B is transmitted through blood, contaminated needles, or sexual contact. Vaccine is recommended for persons providing health care, those who anticipate close contact with the population, and those who plan on extended residence.

Take normal precautions when dealing with animals that bite.

Tip: Order *Tips for Travelers In Mexico*, a pamphlet available from the Superintendent of Documents, U.S. Government Printing Office, Washington, D.C., 20402.

"Once in the town of Todos Santos I saw some guys trying to drive on the beach. They ended up with a car buried in the sand, and a rising tide about to take it away. There was no way to move the car. I wondered what they were doing when I saw some of the local Mexicans in town wheeling empty 55 gallon drums down to the water's edge. They attached the drums to the car, the tide came up and they floated it to shore."
—Goody

Crime: Street crime is common in urban areas, and bandits sometimes roam the countryside in Baja and mainland Mexico. Operations are primarily after dark. Sometimes bandits will disguise themselves as police or other local officials. Report crimes to nearest U.S. Consulate office. It is advised that you not travel on Mexican highways after dark. Check Department of State's pamphlet *"A Safe Trip Abroad."*

If detained or arrested for any reason, contact your embassy and consulate. Call the International Defense Counsel. Phone: (215) 977-9982. They have access to a worldwide network of attorneys. ILDC, Packard Building, 111 S. 15th Street, 24th floor, Philadelphia, PA 19102.

"My friend was drunk in Rosarita, and they took us both to a holding cell with human waste smeared all over the walls. You couldn't sit down, and you couldn't see your hand in front of your face. They do this to try to get you to give them everything you've got. Be patient. They will look into a window every half hour or so, to see how you're doing. Even if you don't feel it, act relaxed. They'll eventually come and give you your fine, unless you've done something really bad. Then you could be there a while."
—From the journal of Randy Dible

A FEW USEFUL WORDS AND PHRASES:
good morning: *buenos dias.*
good afternoon: *buenos tardes.*
good evening: *buenos noches.*
good-bye: *adios*
thank you: *gracias*
please: *por favor*
beer: *cerveza*
water: *agua*
excuse me: *perdoneme*

fire: *fuego*
I am sick: *Estoy enfermo*
help: *auxilo; socorro*
today: *hoy*
tomorrow: *mañana*
What time is it?: *Qué hora es?*
bad: *malo*
good: *bueno*
dirty: *sucio*
cheap: *barato*
clean: *limpio*
difficult: *dificil*
large: *grande'*
passport: *pasaporte*
highway: *carretera*
road: *camino*
hotel: *hotel*
inn: *posada*
room: *cuarto*
kitchen: *cocina*
breakfast: *desayuno*
lunch: *almuerzo*
dinner: *cena*
spoon: *cuchara*
cup: *taza*
knife: *cuchillo*
fork: *tenedor*
chicken: *pollo* (double "l" is pronounced "y")
egg: *huevo*
fish: *pescado*
meat: *carne*
beans: *frijoles*
rice: *arroz*
vegetables: *legumbres*
coffee: *café*
juice: *jugo*
milk: *leche*
tea: *té*

NATURAL HAZARDS: Surprisingly friendly in that department. Still, be aware of rattlesnakes and scorpions on land, stingrays and the occasional shark in the water.

UNNATURAL HAZARDS: Narrow roads with some bad drivers and big trucks on them. Federales, bandits.

FURTHER ON: If you are traveling on to mainland Mexico, the Mexican Government operates ferry service between Baja and the mainland. Round trips connect ports of Santa Rosalia, Guaymas, La Paz, Topolobampo, and Mazatlan. Be sure to make reservations several days in advance, and up to one month in advance during the holiday season.
La Paz. Phone: (68) 25-3833
Santa Rosalia. Phone: (68) 52-0013
Topolobampo. Phone: (68) 62-0035
Guaymas. Phone: (62) 22-3390
Mazatlan. Phone: (67) 81-7020

Cassidy

MAINLAND MEXICO

The Volvo was starting to sputter and smoke. We drove to a little fishing village, and that's where it died. That's also where we found an insane left point. Anyway, we traded the car for a pallapa on the beach, and surfed every day, riding waves from three to ten feet with nobody around but the local fishermen. After a while we went broke and so decided to work on the fishing boats. It was my job to go into the net and take the sharks out. When we made enough money, we quit work again and went back to surfing every day.

For three months we surfed, and then one day I was lying in my hammock and I felt kind of guilty. We gathered up all of our possessions and had a swap meet. Then we had enough money to get back to San Diego on the bus.

—From the journal of surfer, photographer, adventurer, Randy Dible.

FIRST GLIMPSE: Some black and white photos passed around Huntington Pier of a nice left called "Canons" in Mazatlan. I think that the surfer was a Huntington Beach guy named Sam Buel.

BEST SEASON FOR SURF: The biggest waves can be found in the summer months, between late May and late September.

SURFBOARDS: The waves can vary from playful points, to near Pipeline-type barrels breaking over sand. Ideally you would bring a semi gun, a hotdog board, and a longboard. Try to bring at least two boards anyway, one for big surf, the other for gentler days.

OTHER SURF ACCESSORIES: Bring *Solarez* and a repair kit for serious dings like a cracked fin. Waterproof hat, sunglasses, sunscreen with an SPF of 15, or over. Rashguard, first-aid kit, mosquito repellent, mosquito netting, fishing gear, two rolls of good-quality duct tape, vest, thin spring suit optional. Bring at least one extra, heavy-duty leash. Lots of tropical wax. Make sure to bring everything that you need to surf, and spares of some of those things.

Miscellaneous: Bring toilet paper, as much drinking water as you can comfortably carry, a water purification system (check "General Iinformation" in this book for recommended ones), canned food, dried fruit. T-shirts, surf mags, and wax are good gifts for the locals. Bring all types of flashlights, a small portable one, and a big waterproof one. Bring extra batteries. Get two large boxes of matches, the stick variety that light on things like rocks. Store matches in different places. If one box should get wet (anything can happen in Mexico) you still have the other box. Learn some basic Spanish phrases. *Gracias* goes a long way. Also, if you have a video camera, video the locals surfing, and show it to them. They'll be totally stoked, and you might just have a friend for life. There are several hot local surfers in the Puerto Escondido area. Respect them. Of course, you will.

WEATHER: Hot and wet from June-November. Hot and dry from November-May. Humidity runs high along the coast in summer. Things cool down in the mountain regions, and in Mexico City. Generally high 70's F to low 80's F in winter. About 10 degrees hotter in the summer. Wet season is in summer, May through October. Dry season is from November through April. Water temperatures 70 F and above year-round.

Call 1-900-WEATHER.

CROWDS: Only in the well-known regions.

Clothing: Dress for the heat. Bring a nice set of clothes, just in case you want to go to a nice restaurant. Other than that, it's mostly T-shirts, shorts, and sandals. The locals dress casually but conservatively for the most part.

AIR TRANSPORTATION: International airports at: Puerto Valletta, Guadalajara in Jalisco. Mazanillo in Colima.
Puerto Vallarta International Airport (1-12-98, 1, 13-25)
Aero California (1-15-72) has regular, daily flights from Guadalajara, Mazatlan, Phoenix and San Diego.
Alaska Airlines: (3-03, 50, 2-12, 52) daily flights from Los Angeles and San Francisco
American Airlines: (1-17,99, 2-30-19). Flies daily to Dallas.
Delta: 1-19-19, 1-10, 32
Aeromexico and Mexicana: Daily to: Los Angeles, Tijuana, La Paz, Guadalajara, and Mexico City.
Mexicana: (2-50-00, 1-11-38): Daily to Denver, Guadalajara, Los Angeles, Mazatland, San Francisco.

There are daily flights to **Puerto Escondido** from Oaxaca and Mexico City. Crime against tourists is a problem. Travel with friends, especially after dark.

Reservations in hotels may be necessary from December to April, but the biggest surf is likely between May through October, so who really cares?

DOCUMENTS: All visitors going much farther south than Ensenada, must have a passport, and a *Mexican Government Tourist Card.* Try to bring a birth certificate, or notarized copy of your birth certificate, voter's registration card, or military discharge papers. Have your papers in order, and keep them in the same place, where they can be readily shown to officials. Tourist cards are available at no charge from the Mexican Consulates, embassies, and immigration, several auto clubs, and travel agents. Tourist cards are good for 90 days. Anyone under 18 must have a notarized letter of authorization from both parents.

The driver of the car will also need an auto permit (ask your travel agent). The auto permit doubles as the driver's tourist card. It is illegal to sell your car in Mexico. Make sure that you get adequate Mexican insurance, which is available along the border, through the auto club or from a Mexican insurance agent (check entry under "Insurance").

Entering mainland Mexico either from Tijuana, San Diego or Los Angeles requires a visa. Visas are good for 30, 60 and 90 days. Also, you will need to have a major credit card.   •

If you are traveling by car, make sure that it's in good condition (although some hellmen like Randy Dible have made it down deep in absolute beaters.) Whether you are entering at Nogales, Arizona, or through La Paz by ferry from Baja, you will need to have all of your papers in good order. (Theoretically visas are required beyond Ensenada, but this is rarely enforced in Baja.)

Tip: Make sure that the gas gauge on the pump is set at zero when pumping. You're more likely to get the best gas in the larger towns.

In the 60's, Kemp Aaberg wrote a bitchin' story about driving to Mazatlan. A few years later, Ron Stoner went down with Tom Leonardo and Jack Cantou. They named the place "Stoner's," (not because of the state of the surfers who went there, but after legendary surf photographer, Ron Stoner.)

GROUND TRANSPORTATION: If you drive the entire Baja Peninsula, take the ferry across. Make reservations for the ferry in season.

Cars entering Mexico are subject to search without probable cause. Firearms are prohibited, except during hunting season, and then only with the proper permits.

Reserving a rental car from abroad:
Cars average from about U.S. $45 a day
Hertz: (800) 654-3131
National: (800) 328-4567
Budget: (800) 527-0700
Avis: (800) 331-2112

Driving can be nuts, and the rules seem to change depending upon who's giving out the tickets. Roadside assistance: The *Green Angels* are roadside mechanics in bright green trucks. They'll give you gas, a jump start, and can do small repairs. All for free. What a country!

Most driver's licenses are valid. Bring an octane booster, available at American auto parts store.
Driving is challenging even under the best of circumstances. Road signs are often randomly placed, traffic in the cities is fast and crowded, the roads are often poorly maintained.

INSURANCE: See "Insurance Section" under Baja.

CURRENCY EXCHANGE: One U.S. dollar = 5.549 peso. *Exchange rates will fluctuate.*

ELECTRICAL CURRENT: 110V, 60 cycles AC

LODGING: There are not many youth hostels in coastal mainland Mexico. However, if you buy a *Youth Plan Card*, you can receive numerous discounts throughout Mexico. For information, phone: 525-26-99, 525-29-74, 525-21-53.

For student discounts write to: *Association Mexicana de Albergues de la Juventud*, AC, Avenida Francisco I Madero No 6, Despachos 314 y 315, Mexico 1, DF.

Youth Hostel:
Zihuatanejo
Ave Paseo de las Salinas s/n Zihuatanejo
Gro, CP 40880
Phone: 44662
Cost $15,000 pesos
Make reservations at least 15 days in advance

Camping:
Mazatlan:
Tents can be pitched at any of the trailer parks, but the prices range between U.S. $16 and U.S. $20. Also, there are hordes of RVs with loud generators and VCRs blasting the sit-coms you so desperately tried to escape. There is free camping at the end of Avenida Camar'on Sa'balo, but be careful of theives.

San Blas:
The Trailer Park Los Cocos
Phone: (321) 5-00-55

Electricity and showers available.
Mosquitoes are also available, especially after dark.

Hotels:
There are numerous good, inexpensive hotels in Mexico.
The following is a partial list:

Mazatlan:
Hotel Del Centro
Phone: (67) 81-26-73
With fans, from U.S. $10-U.S. $13

Bargain basement:
The Hotel Mexico
Phone: (67) 81-38-06
For those who want to save money and don't mind the
occasional hole in the wall.
U.S. $9

Hotel San Jorge
Phone: (67) 81-36-95
Across from the beach
U.S. $12.50-U.S. $15

San Blas
Posada Porola
Phone: (321) 5-03-81
Good sized bungalows with cooking facilities.
U.S. $20

Hotel Posada del Rey
Phone: (321) 5-01-23
Fans, hot water, swimming pool.
US $17-U.S $27

Hotel Flaminigos
U.S. $15-U.S. $18

Casa de Playa Acxali
Phone: (958) 2-02-78
Sparce, but adequate. Cabanas for up to four people.
Mosquito nets, fans, fridge, showers and filtered water.
Cost: About U.S. $13. There are other cabanas in the
area: Rockaway, and Las Olas are considered decent.
About U.S. $10

Perez Gasga
Phone: (958) 2-01-59
U.S. $8.50-U.S. $11.50—the low price is reflective of
the quality.

Playa Marinero
Hotel Arco Iris
Phone: (958) 2-04-32
Clean, fan-cooled rooms. Looks into the surf. Pool,
bar, restaurant. You're on it. US $16.25 -U.S.$20

FOOD: There is inexpensive food throughout the country. Fresh fish is readily available, as are fruits and vegetables. Be careful of the raw vegetables. Make sure
that pork and chicken are well cooked. Be sure that
you peel any fruit yourself, unless it's served in a nice
restaurant or hotel. Check to see that everything is clean
if you plan on eating things like ceviche'.

WATER: Drink bottled water.

PHONES: International Code: (96) Country code: (52)
City Codes: Mexico City: (5). Puerto Vallarta: (322).
Puerto Escondido: (958).

MEDICAL CARE: Get the Harvix shot described in
the "General Information" section, for Hepatitis A, a
common ailment afflicting many surfers in Mexican waters.

There are hospitals and clinics in most of the cities. If you have a major medical problem, it might be best to wait until you get to a major city for treatment.

- **Montezuma's Revenge** (a severe case of diarrhea). You'll be losing it from both ends, and sure that you're going to die. It's doesn't last long, and it will probably get better in a day or two. Take it easy, replenish fluids, avoid dairy products.

  To avoid Montezuma's Revenge avoid salads, unpasturized milk and cheese, raw or rare meats, fish, shellfish. Make sure that meals are freshly cooked and served hot. Drink only beverages from sealed cans and bottles. *Pepto Bismol* should relieve the symptoms.

  While the local people don't seem to have any problems with the water, don't assume that this will work for you. Make sure that water has been boiled for at least 20 minutes or purified. Water purifiers are a good thing to carry. Check major outdoor stores, like *REI* or *A-16*. Also, check the "General Information" section in this book.

- **Cholera is present.** Cholera vaccine not required or recommended. Strict adherence to food and water precautions will help to lowers risks.
- **Malaria is present.** Take normal precautions against mosquito bites.
- Update tetanus/diphtheria, measles/ mumps/ rubella, and polio vaccines as appropriate to age and date of last dose. Harvix for Hepatitis A (Check "General Information" section of this book.) Typhoid vaccine is recommended for travelers visiting areas other than major resorts, and who are anticipating extended stays.
- **Hepatitis B**: Transmitted through blood, contaminated needles, or sexual contact. Vaccine is recommended for persons providing health care, those who

anticipate close contact with population, and those who plan on extended residence.

- **Rabies:** Take normal precautions when dealing with animals that bite.
- **STD's:** Take normal precautions.

Adequate **medical care** can be found in all major cities. Health facilities in Mexico City are excellent. Care in remote areas is limited. Air pollution in Mexico City can be harsh. Additional health information is available from the *Center for Disease Control's* international travelers hotline at (404) 332-4559.

Caution: Some of the Federales will wave you over and then just sit there, waiting for you to approach them. Get out of your car, and bring them money, U.S. $20 is the usual, and if you've got the nerve, you might even be able to barter your way into a lower fine. (As far as I know, Dible holds the record for being pulled over, five times on one trip out of Mexico City). If you are asked to follow a Federales to the courthouse, don't argue.

Be watchful of your vehicle when you are pulled over. The federales are looking for guns or illegal drugs. Don't panic, but make sure that nothing is planted on you or your vehicle, something that some Mexican cops have been reputed to do at times. Don't travel with anyone carrying illegal drugs. Bandits can be a problem south of Michoacan. Be careful, and cooperative. On single-lane bridges, the first approaching driver to flick his headlights has right-of-way. Driving after dark is not advised. The police may be corrupt, but you're better off falling into their hands that those of the bandits, who do, on rare occasions kill people. I was once held at gun-point once by a 16-year-old, in a remote region.

A dog can be good protection from bandits or

federales. Make sure that you have two certificates from a vet stating that the dog is in good health and has had a rabies shot within the last six months.

Be careful traveling at night. Livestock often jump into the road, and big tractor-trailers can be a nightmare. The AAA can inform you of road and bridge conditions in advance.

Tip: Bring someone along to sacrifice to the mosquitoes. It seems that they'll pick one person to feed on, and leave the others alone.

Tip: Bring along some broken appliances, and keep them on the seat. When pulled over by the federales offer them your broken camera, VCR, or other junk. They might just take it.

Haggling is expected. Negotiate prices for most items bought from stores. It's part of the fun.

POSTAL: It is advised that you get mail sent to a private address. If you need to have mail sent to the post office, however, try to make sure that it's a major post office. When having mail sent, put the last name first, all in upper case. *Registered Mail* would be the safest bet. Check for an *American Express* office to receive your mail.

CRIME: Pick-pockets are found in the usual areas: crowded buses and trains, shopping malls. Robberies can occur on the road or in the cities. Give them what they want, and you probably won't get hurt. Bandits sometimes cruise the countryside.

Tip: Don't eat the seafood if the sea is a long ways from the fish being served.

127

Local customs: This is a very religious country, deeply rooted in family values. Still, the locals love a fiesta. Be reverent and observant of their ways, and you'll have a better time.

Traditions: Mexicans seem to have invented family values and have a deep sense of devotion. Common courtesy and reverence for all things Catholic is important. Also, wear shirts and shoes when in public. Don't spit on sidewalks, get too loud, or debate the local politics.

A FEW USEFUL WORDS AND PHRASES:
See Baja section. (Some words may be pronouned differently in various regions.)

NATURAL HAZARDS:
No see ums, mosquetos, stingrays, jellyfish, occassionally sharks.

UNNATURAL HAZARDS:
Some of the regions are extremely wild. Be careful when driving through them. Bandits carry guns, especially in "growers" regions.

Dible

COSTA RICA

FIRST GLIMPSE: *Some pretty, but blurry pictures that my brother took in 1970.*

BEST SEASON FOR SURF: Good waves can be found throughout the year. A good variety, mostly Southern California-type waves.

SURFBOARDS: Anything goes. Mostly hotdog boards, and longboards. A semi-gun isn't a bad idea for the bigger days. Bring the board you generally use for small to medium waves. You'll find a lot of variety and good reef waves. The surf can, however, get hollow.

OTHER SURF ACCESSORIES: No wetsuits needed. Rashguard (preferably long sleeved). Vest is optional. Booties, for some shallow reefs are also an option. Bring lots of tropical wax. Sunscreen with an SPF of at least 15. Possibly waterproof hat, and goggles. There are several surf shops in Costa Rica. Around San José, Check *Mango Surf Shop* Phone: 25-1067
   Caution: The water can be extremely polluted near the cities. Be careful when surfing rivermouths.

WEATHER: Two seasons: wet and dry. Pretty hot all year long. Dry season goes from December through April. Everything else is considered the wet season, and you quickly find out why everything there is so green. It can rain an average of 20 days per month in the wet times. Rain can occur nearly any time of year.

Clothing: Casual and conservative. Bring something for the rain.

CROWDS: Only at the main breaks.

AIR TRANSPORTATION: Juan Santamaria International Airport, a few miles outside of San José, is where the international flights arrive. Cheaper fares will often make numerous stops along the way to Costa Rica, and a flight from the U.S. can go through Texas, Florida and Mexico City. What should be about a five-hour flight becomes a 14-hour flight.

The Costa Rican airline, *Lacsa,* offers discounts to teachers and college staff. Contact OTEC Phone: 22-0866 Fax: 33-2321. Calle 3, Avenida 3, San José.

Remember that the best deals on airline tickets can be had if you purchase your ticket in advance. Stand-by tickets can be a bargain for those with time on their hands.

Check the Sunday "travel section" of the newspaper, and the "General Information" section of this book under the "Air Transportation" entry.

Sometimes airfare will be given free from *Lacsa Airlines* to photographers or journalists who can show a strong portfolio, and prove that they are going to give positive exposure to Costa Rica in a publication. There are numerous package tours to Costa Rica, many of which are advertised in *Surfer* and *Surfing Magazines.* *Surf Express* is a popular one.

Airlines:
Aero Costa Rica: (800) 237-6274
Lacsa: (800) 225-2272
Aviateca: (800) 327-9832
Taca: (800) 535-8780
American: (800) 433-7300
Continental: (800) 525-0280
United: (800) 722-5243

DOCUMENTS: A 90-day stay in Costa Rica is allowed without a visa for citizens of Canada, France, Japan, Panama, Spain, most eastern European countries, Mexico, Brazil, Australia, New Zealand, France and the U.S. A valid passport is required. Visas are not required if the applicant is planning on staying 30 days or less. Visas for other nationalities can be obtained through the Costa Rican Consulate, or your travel agent. Visa extensions can be obtained with some difficulty within the country. Perhaps an easier method is to leave the country for 72 hours or more, and then re-apply. Your travel agent can advise you and help you with this.

GROUND TRANSPORTATION: *It's a long ride, sometimes dangerous, but, I am told, a hell of an adventure to drive to Costa Rica. In 1973 my brother Dave, bought a used Pontiac GTO from Donald Takayama, packed up and headed south. Just out of Tijuana, he was in a wreck that nearly killed him. By the time he arrived in Costa Rica, however, his luck had changed, and the 'Ticos" were so glad to see the then unusual sight of an American surfer, that they treated him royally. The way he describes that trip, I'm surprised that he ever came back.*

The railway system links the capital, San José, with the major port of Puntarenas. The railway system in Limón has been discontinued, but is available through the Atlantic lowlands. Trains are old, but inexpensive. Buses go just about everywhere, and are inexpensive, clean and on time. Schedules are available at the *Tourma Hostel* or at the *Tourist Board Information Center* at the Plaza de la Cultura (Avenida Central, Calle 3).

     Ferry is the best way to get to Nicoya Peninsula from Puntarenas or points east and south.

     Rental cars are a good idea, and Jeeps are probably the best bet, especially if you want to cover any ground, something which is necessary since the major surf spots in Costa Rica can be half a day apart. Enjoy the long, winding road. The place is beautiful.

Caution: When driving, try to avoid night travel. Roads can be rough. Day travel from the U.S., to Costa Rica could take about a week if you go straight through from Brownsville, Texas. The big delays are at the border crossings, which can be an exercise in frustration. Carry good insurance. Have your papers in good order. Look clean. Don't carry illegal substances. Don't leave your car unattended. Bring spare parts and tools. Have your car checked out by a mechanic before you go.

It's better to get a taxi through San José than try to negotiate the traffic on your own in a rented car. If you do rent a car upon arrival, check it carefully for dents, tires and damage that might already be there. *U-Haul Rent-A-Car,* not an affiliate of *U-Haul International,* has a reputation equal to the major rent-a-car companies for reliability.

LANGUAGE: Primarily Spanish. A lot of people speak good English, and the children are educatated in both Spanish and English. Check Baja section for a few words and pharases

CURRENCY EXCHANGE: One U.S. dollar = 153. 68 colones. *Exchange rates will fluctuate.*

Master Card and *Visa* are widely accepted, but you will need some local currency. You can purchase Costa Rican currency in a major bank.

LODGING: While prices have jumped substantially in recent years, food and lodging are still a bargain in Costa Rica. First-class hotels can go up to $100 a day, but you can find an adequate place to sleep for about $10.

- Guanacaste-Coco Beach Hostel
  Playas del Coco, Guanacaste
  Phone: 22-1037
  Cost: U.S. $ 13.50
- Hotel Nuevo Internatcional
  Phone: 58-0662
  U.S. $ 12.50
- Tamarindo
  Pozo Azul
  Phone: 67-4380
  U.S. $ 21- U.S. $27
- Quepos
  Hotel Luna
  Phone: 77 0012
  U.S. $ 4.50

FOOD: Good food at a good price. Lots of fish, rice and black beans. Uncooked foods such as salads and fruits should be avoided, unless you can peel the fruit yourself.

WATER: In some beach areas, water should be bottled or purified. Generally water is okay in and around major towns. Still, you might want to boil or filter it in the more remote regions. Soft drinks, beer, and bottled water are not hard to find. Avoid ice, except in major hotels.

Banks are open from 9 a.m. - 3 p.m. At the central offices in San José, they are open from 8:30 a.m.- 5:30 p.m.

PHONES: The telephone system in Costa Rica is the best in Latin America, and there are more phones here than in any other country in Central America. Look for the telephone symbol. Country code: (506). There are no city codes in Costa Rica. Long distance operator: 116. Long distance information: 124. Local information: 113. Emergencies: 911. Police Department: 117. Fire Department: 118.

MEDICAL CARE: "**It**" happens. If you get a case of diarrhea, don't panic. *Pepto Bismol* will relieve most of the symptoms. Work into the food slowly, eating only familiar things at first. Avoid unwashed fruits and vegetables and you'll probably be all right.

Insects are a problem. Mosquito nets, long pants, long sleeve shirts, and insect repellent should be on the list. As mentioned in "General Information", *"Skin So Soft,"* by *Avon,* is considered the best repellent by some hard-core travelers. If bitten, the old calamine lotion or soaking in baking soda is good for relief.

Prostitution is legal in Costa Rica. Female prostitutes receive regular checkups, but there's no sure safe way except abstinence. While condoms decrease risk to a certain extent, they are not 100 per cent safe. Condoms are available in most Costa Rican pharmacies.

Free emergency medical care is provided for everyone through the social security hospitals. Try *San José Hospital de Dios.* Phone: 22-0166. Clinics are also available throughout the country in the main cities. Most prescription drugs can be purchased in the pharmacies. Most doctors expect payment up front. If you have insurance, bill your insurance company upon your return home. Malaria Prophylaxis is recommended, and anything you can think of to keep away bugs.

Miscelaneous: Costa Rica has become a primary destination for surfers from California, Europe, Texas and the East Coast of the U.S. What was once an undiscovered paradise is now a discovered paradise, and you will find many Americans living down there, surfing, hanging out, swirling the ice in their glass and generally trying to pretend like they're the star of a James Bond movie. Still, the place is covered with good surf, friendly people, and lots to see and do. Flights from the U.S. are relatively cheap, and so is lodging. Most of the youth hostels are located inland, but, as mentioned, good, inexpensive lodging can be found near good surf.

I had been traveling with my good friend Bob Miles, in Australia, when he decided to move to Costa Rica. This was in the early '70s , and we all thought that this was a foolish move on Bob's part. We figured that he'd soon be back in Encinitas, working as a bellman to make enough money to get back to Oz. Well, Bob never came home. The last time I checked, he had a fleet of fishing boats, was married to a beautiful Costa Rican woman, and was extremely happy. Okay, I admit it, we blew it, Bob.

POSTAL: Most of the bigger towns have post offices and keep regular hours. Receive mail through Correo Central. San José has the best record for getting mail on time (it takes about a week from the U.S.) For mail received, put your last name all in caps. Parcels sent from overseas are held until duty is paid. This can be time consuming. Check for an *American Express* office to receive mail.

Film is expensive here, so bring a good stash from home.

Tip: Good maps can be obtained through the *Costa Rican National Tourist Bureau.*

CRIME: There has been an increase in crime, and some-times you can get into trouble, mostly from pick- pockets and the occasional robbery.

Miscellaneous: There are two methods for seeing a country: One is to stay in the same place the entire time and gain a more intimate knowledge of one region. The other is to travel about looking for the best surf. In Costa Rica, the surf spots can be far apart. Still, when the surf isn't happening, there's plenty to do. A drive in just about any direction will yield fantastic scenery. Fishing's good on the day boats.

Costa Rica is an extremely progressive country, with a high literacy rate and relatively low crime. Twenty-seven per cent of the country is protected against the developers tractor, which are certainly on the move in unprotected areas. The land boom is basically over for now, and cheap acreage is no longer available like it was before the country made appearances on the six o'clock news, and *Jurassic Park*.

While **women** are generally held in higher es-teem than in other parts of Latin America, you still need to be cautious if traveling alone. Try to ignore men who make advances, unless, of course...

NATURAL HAZARDS: Nothing much, really. Mos-quitoes are pretty gnarly, so avoid unscreened areas after dark. Occasional critters that bite or sting in the water. Some sharks. Snakes and spiders on the Gulf side.

UNNATURAL HAZARDS: Some of the surf spots can be extremely polluted. Ask around, and be cautious when surfing rivermouths, or near population centers.

FURTHER ON: Nicaragua: Nowhere near as mellow as Costa Rica. Good surf to be had. A nice place broken down by years of war. Regulations for entry are subject to change, so check before you go. Visas are available in San José, and take about two days to process. Also, check to see if there are travel advisories in the area. Nicaragua can be entered from Costa Rica by crossing the southern border. At this time, residents of the U.S. and Canada are not required to hold visas while visiting Nicaragua.

Panama: Visas are required if you are from U.S., Japan, Canada, Australia, New Zealand, and most European counties except for the UK, and a few others. Check with Panamanian Consulate for requirements. Visas can be obtained in San José, through your travel agent, or at the border crossing.

Brewer

AUSTRALIA

FIRST GLIMPSE: *Some weird shots of the Fairy Bower in Surfer Magazine. Ten years after: Kirra, 1972 — A four-foot swell, slightly onshore, sitting behind Michael Peterson, watching him take off and weave through the bowl for another long barrel.*

BEST SEASON FOR SURF: November through February is generally the biggest, but good, solid surf can be found any time of year.

SURFBOARDS: Just about everything. Mostly a board that works in fun surf in the 4-to-6 foot range. Think California with a bit more power.

OTHER SURF ACCESSORIES: At its coldest, which is Victoria (actually Tasmania, if you count that, is even colder in winter) you will need a good fullsuit, and maybe booties. In the Australian summer, it's strictly trunks and rashguards anywhere north of New South Wales. Everything you'll need can be provided by one of the many surf shops that dot the coast. Prices are somewhat higher than in the continental U.S., however, so it might be a good idea to bring all the gear you'll need from home.

AIR TRANSPORTATION: Arrival: Usually Sydney by air. Brisbane, Melbourne and Perth also have international facilities.

Sydney is a large city, complete with water pollution, smog and crime comparable to the "Kojak" years in the U.S. The no-gun law makes it a lot mellower.
Cheap Airfare: Check Sunday newspaper "travel section.." Fiji, Bali, New Zealand—the number of cheap stops going there or back is intriguing. Round-trip or

proof of further travel is needed. Check "Air Transportation" entry under the "General Information" section of this book.

DOCUMENTS: U.S. citizens must have a passport which is good for three months beyond time of intended stay. Also, you need to have a ticket bound for American soil, proof of sufficient funds, and a visa, which can be obtained quickly and easily within about 24 hours.

A valid passport is required by all except New Zealand passport holders. Visas are required for most everyone else. Stay up to three months. No fee. Or apply for a four- year multiple-entry visa, which can be renewed by leaving the country for places like Bali or New Zealand, for a while. Twelve-month working holiday visas are also available, but are difficult to obtain. Honolulu is a good place to apply. Working holiday visas are most often granted to those who can prove that they can fill a position that is needed in Australia. Apply in person or through the mail to your nearest Australian Consulate or Australian Embassy.

Tip: The visa office in LA. is the absolute worst, and it is unlikely that you will encounter more rude, rubber-stamp bureaucrats any place this side of Devil's Island. San Francisco is better. Honolulu is downright pleasant. While a standard tourist visa is easy to obtain, a multiple-entry visa is much better if you plan on spending any time traveling. The visa requires that you leave the country for more than a 24-hour period, once every six months. (This means — damn the luck — that you might "have" to go to Bali or New Zealand on occasion).

The Australian Consulate in Los Angeles is located at: 611 Larchmont Blvd., Los Angeles, CA 92004. Phone: (213) 469-4300. New York: 636 Fifth Ave.,

New York, NY 1011, Phone: (212) 245-4000. Honolulu: (808) 524-5050.

GROUND TRANSPORTATION: Australian auto registration is extremely expensive, but a large part of the cost goes toward insuring the vehicle. All of the cars require registration (regio) tags on them. If you plan on buying a car in Australia, make sure to check that it has a lot of time left on the registration. If not, be sure that you know how much registration for the vehicle will cost.

If you are traveling very far beyond the cities, especially into Western Australia, it is recommended that your car have a "roo bar" attached to it. These metallic bars attached to the front of the car help to prevent the car from being mashed by hitting a kangaroo, believe it or not, a fairly common occurrence out west.

Check out *YHA Greyhound Pioneer Coaches*. They travel most of the main routes throughout Australia. It's called *"Travel Oz."* A 12-month pass can be purchased in or outside of Australia.

City buses take surfboards at the discretion of the drivers. Trains and subways are common modes of transportation. The ferry goes across the harbor.

It may be best to wait to rent a car, especially if you are new to driving on the left side of the road. Most surfers do not come to Australia to surf Sydney, and a trip either north to the Gold Coast, south to Bells, or west, to Margaret River is suggested. If you are planning on driving to Western Australia, make sure that you have a good car, with an especially good radiator. The Nullabor Plain gets extremely hot, and there's not much shade.

Cars are expensive, and the bare minimum will be about $1,000. Falcons and Holden station wagons are fairly reliable, and they are big enough to sleep in, if need be. Cheap cars can be located at backpackers' regions, in the newspapers, or anywhere that travelers congregate. Like anywhere else, you are likely to find a deal if someone is leaving in a hurry. Also, the auto auctions in Sydney are good places to get cheap cars. U.S. and Canadian licenses are valid, but it's not a bad idea to have an International Driver's License. Some of the rental car companies prefer them.

All of the major car rental companies are highly visible.

Petrol throughout Australia is about $3 a U.S. gallon. It's sold by the liter, so don't be fooled by the apparently low price.

CURRENCY EXCHANGE: One U.S. dollar = 1.30 Australian dollars. The airport is not the best place to exchange money, so try the *American Express* office on King Street in Sydney. Rates of exchange vary from place to place. *Exchange rates will fluctuate.*

ELECTRICAL CURRENT: 240 V, 50 cycle through-out Australia. If you have any electronic devices like a hair dryer, power planer, or computer that you want to bring from home, check three-pronged adapters and transformers in the "Electrical Current" entry, under "General Information."

LODGING:
Youth Hostel Credit Card Booking
Phone: 02 261 1111

Youth Hostels:
Airlie Beach
394 Shute Harbor Road, Queensland 4802.
Phone: (79) 466-312 - $13- $16

Albany
49 Duke St.
Albany, Western Australia 6330
Phone: (98) 413-949

Ballina
Traveler's Lodge, 36 Tamar St., Ballina, NSW 2478
Phone/fax: (66) 866-737- $13-$15

Beachport
Beachport, South Australia 5280
Phone: (87) 358-197 - $8

Bicheno
Bicheno, Tasman Highway, Tasmania 7215
Phone: (3) 751-293 - $9

Brisbane
Brisbane Gardens
15 Mitchell St, Kedron, Queensland 4031
Phone: (7) 857-1245 - $12

Bruny Island
"Lumeah," Quiet Corner, Main Road, Adventure Bay,
Tasmania 7150
Phone: (02) 93 - 1265 - $13

Bunbury
Corner of Sterling & Moore Streets
Bunbury, Western Australia 6230
Phone: (97) 912-621 - $11

Byron Bay
Cape Byron Hostel
Corner of Byron & Middleton St.
Byron Bay, NSW 2481
Phone: (66) 858-788 Fax: (66) 858-788

Byron Bay
Cape Byron Lodge
78 Bangalow Rd., Byron Bay, NSW 2481
Phone/fax: (66) 856-445 $11-$15

Carnarvon
Backpacker's Paradise,
 10 Robinson Street, Carnarvon,
 Western Australia 6701
Phone: (99) 412-966

Coffs Harbour
Albany Street, Coffs Harbour, NSW 2405
Phone/fax: (66) 526-462-$12-$15

Coles Bay
Freyciner National Park,
 Coles Bay, Tasmania 7215
Phone: c/o (02) 349-617 - $7

Western Australia
Coolgardie
Gnarlbine Rd, Coogardie
Western Australia 6429
Phone: (90) 266-051 - $11

Denmark
Wilson Inlet Holiday Park
Ocean Beach Rd, Denmark
Western Australia 6333
Phone: (98) 481-267 - $11

Dunsborough
Geographe Bay Rd
Quindalup, Western Australia 6282
Phone: (97) 553-107 - $13

Esperance
Goldfields Rd, Esperance
Western Australia 6450
Phone: (90) 711-040 - $11

Exmouth
Exmouth Backpackers
Exmouth Cape Tourist Village
Truscott Cres, Exmouth
Western Australia 6707
Phone: (99) 491-101 - From $12

Geraldton
Peninsula Backpackers
311 Marine Terrace, Geraldton
Western Australia 6530
Phone: (99) 214-770 - $11

Margaret River
Margaret River Lodge YHA
220 Railway Terrace, Margaret River
Western Australia 6285
Phone: (97) 572-532 - $12

Nannup Black Cockatoo, 27
Grange Rd., Nannup
Western Australia 6275
Phone: 561-035 - $11

Perth
Scarborough Beach,
Mandarin Gardens Hostel
20-28 Wheatcroft St
Scarborough, Perth
Phone: (9) 341-5431 - Fax: (9) 245-1553
$11

South Australia
Flinders National Park
Oraparinna & Gammon Ranges
Via Hawker South Australia 5434
Phone: (86) 484-244 - $11

Port Vincent
On Girl Guide Property
Port Vincent, South Australia
Phone: (88) 537-285 or 537-030 - $6.50

New South Wales
Forester
Dolphin Lodge, 43 Head Street
Forester, NSW 2428
Phone: (65) 558-155-$14-$19

Garie Beach
Royal National Park
NSW
Phone: (2) 261-1111-$ 6

Port Macquarie
40 Church Street, Port Macquarie
New South Wales 2444
Phone: (65) 835-512 - $12-$13

Newcastle
Irene Hall, 27 Pacific St., Newcastle
New South Wales 2300
Phone: (49) 293-324
Fax: (49) 297-775 - $13-$20

Sydney
Hereford Lodge
51 Hereford St., Glebe
NSW 2037
Phone: (2) 660-5577 - $16-$24

Victoria
Lorne
Great Ocean Road Backpackers
10 Erskine Ave, Lorne, Victoria
3232. Phone: (52) 891-809 - $15

Philip Island
Amaroo Park
97 Church St, Cowes
Philip Island, Victoria 3922
Phone: (59) 522-548 - $10

Queensland
Gold Coast
Cooangatta Rd, Bilinga
Queensland 4225
Phone: (75) 367-644 - $12.-$15

Great Keppel Island
Keppel YH, Captain Cook Memorial
Lion's Camp, Great Keppel Island
Queensland 4703
Phone: (79) 275-288 - $13-$15

Maroochydore
Holiday Hostile, 24 Schirrmann Drive
Marochydore, Queensland 4558
Phone: (74) 433-151 - $12-14

Mission Beach
"Treehouse Hostel"
Bingal Bay Road, Mission Beach
North Queensland 4854
Phone: (70) 687-137 - $14

Tasmania
Hobart
52 King St
Bellerive, Hobart, Tasmania 7018
Phone: (02) 442-552 - $10

Mount Field National Park
Main Road, Mt. Field National Park
Tasmania 7140
Phone: (02) 881-369 - $11

Cygnet
Balfes Hill, Cradoc Road
Cradoc, Tasmania 7109
Phone: (02) 951-551 - $12

Boards for Hire: Some youth hostels provide complimentary surfboards to their guests, but don't count on it. The best thing, of course, is to have your own board. If you can't do that, and the hostels don't have boards to your liking, many of the surf shops will hire boards by the day.

Camping: Much of the camping in Australia is done at what are called "Caravan Parks." A caravan is what Americans generally refer to as a trailer. Many caravan parks rent caravans by the night. Some offer tent camping, and cabin rentals also. Camping is extremely popular throughout Australia. Christmas, Easter and the entire month of January will usually require reservations far in advance.

North Coast
Stocton Beach Caravan Park
Phone: 049 28 1393 - $9

There are several Caravan Parks south of Newcastle, around Redhead Beach.

Bombah Point, Myall Shores
Phone: 049 974-495.
Tent sites $13/Cabins $40

Byron Bay Area
First Sun Caravan Park
Phone: 06 85-6544
Tent camping sites start at $8 with a $4 charge for each
additional person.

Clark's Beach Caravan Park
Phone: 066 85-6496
Sites are a little more expensive than other parks, but
cabins are only $27.

Suffolk Park Caravan Park
Phone: 066 85-3353 - $8-$9

Broken Head
Phone: 066 85-3245 - $8-$9

South Coast
Corrimal
Phone: 042-85-5688/ About $12 per night
$40 for cabins.

Bulli
Farrell Road
Phone: 042-855-477 - $12 per night/$40 for cabins

Windang Island
Phone: 042-97-3166 - $12 per night/$40 cabins

Depot Beach
Moore's Caravan Park
Phone: 044-78-6010 - Starts at $ 4

Pebbly Beach
Phone: 044-78-6006
Tent sites $10 - $7.50 per additional person.

Queensland
Amity Point.   Accessible only by 4WD
Phone: 07-409-8192-$8

Point Lookout
Thankful Rest Camp Ground
Phone: 07-409-8192
Tent sites, $8

Stradbroke Island Caravan Park
Phone: 07-409-8127
Tent sites, $8 and up

Main Beach Caravan Park
Phone: 075-81-7722
No tent sites. Cabins, about $35

Loaders Creek Tourist Park
Phone: 075-01-7733
Tent sites: $10/Cabins $35

Border Caravan Park
Phone: 075-36-3134 - Tent sites, $11

The Content Caravan Park
Phone: 074-49-7746

Sunrise Holiday
Phone: 074-47-3294
Tent sites, about $12

Dilli Village Recreational Camp
Phone: 071-27-9130
Tent Sites, $3-Cabins: $40

Tourist Park
Phone: 085-552-144
Kessell Road
Tent sites, $8 and up/Vans: $20-$30

The Corrong
Need Prior Permit
Phone: 085-75-7014 - $3 and up

Moonta Bay Caravan Park
Phone: 088-25-2406
Powered sites from $14/Cabins from $46

Streaky Bay
The Coffin Bay Caravan Park
Phone: 086- 85- 4176 or 086-85-4170
Tent sites from about $12

Tasmania:
Sandy Bay Caravan Park
Tent sites: $10. Powered sites, $12. Cabins, $32

Point Arthur Point Caravan Park
Phone: 022-50-2340
Tent sites: $9. Cabins: $45

Treasure Island Caravan Park
Phone: 033-44-2600
Tent sites: 9. Vans: $32. Cabins: $42

Mole Creek Camp Ground
Phone: 003-63-1102
Tent sites: $4

West Stanan Caravan Park
Phone: 004-71-7239
Tent sites: $8

Victoria
Zeally Bay Caravan Park
Phone: 052-61-2400
Tent sites: $12/Vans: $32

Pisces Caravan Park
Phone: 052-37-6749
Tent sites: $13. Vans: $30

Surfside One Caravan Park
Phone: 055-61-2611
Tent sites: $12

Mallacota Camping Park
Phone: 051-58-0300
Tent sites: $8

Western Australia
Cactus:
No phone number available
Bring your own water. Watch for sharks.
Tent sites: $4

Busselton Caravan Park
Phone: 097-52-1175
Tent sites: $10

River View Caravan Park
Phone: 097-57-2270
Tent sites: About $ 12

Middletonwn Beach Caravan Park
Phone: 098-41-4616
Tent sites: About $10

Separation Point
Phone: 099-21-2763
Tents and vans available.

Denham
Denham Seaside Caravan Park
Phone: 099-48-1242
Tent sites: From $10/Vans: $32

Carnarvon
Carnarvon Tourist Center Caravan Park
Phone: 099-41-2966
Tent sites: $12/Vans: $25

Exmouth Caravan Park
Phone: 099-49-1331
Tent sites: $12

Lodge Caravan Park
Phone: 099-49-1908
Tent sites: $12-$15

Tip: In general you will find Australians quick to pack up for a week of exploring the country side. They are proud to show you their surf spots, so leave your maps of the surf spots at home, and enjoy the ride.

FOOD: All food is fit for human consumption, but nutritional value is at times questionable. Good, fried junk food abounds. Fruits and vegetables are also plentiful throughout the country. Cheap eats at "milk bars" which serve some great grease and sugar— milk shakes and assorted other crap. There are all sorts of good "take out" international foods, like Indian, which are inexpensive for the most part. Not many great restaurants, especially beyond Sydney. If you are eating in an Australian restaurant, and plan to actually sit at a table, there is a surcharge of about 15 percent.

Tip: If someone "shouts" (buys) a round of beers, it is expected that you will do the same.

WATER: Decent drinking water comes from the tap in nearly all regions of Australia. Many people prefer bottled drinking water for health and taste, however.

Tip: If you plan on drinking in an Australian pub, you had better practice with some real Australian beer before going there. Otherwise, you won't be able to keep up. Australian beer is a lot stronger than most domestic beers in the U.S.

Tip: The pub is often the cheapest place in town to get a good meal.

PHONES: Country code (61) City codes: Sydney (2) Perth (9) Adalaide (8) Brisbane (7) Melbourne (3)

Work: There are numerous illegal Yanks in Australia, and it's not really too difficult to find a job illegally since much of the young population is collecting the dole.

REGIONAL CHARACTERISTICS:
The South Coast consists of small towns, strung together by some very good, hard breaking, and sometimes wild reef breaks. The waves are similar to lightweight North Shore spots—fast, hollow, shallow. The surfers are generally aggressive, and more than competent. Show them respect, and there's no worries. There is a good train system out of Sydney that serves many of the South Coast towns. Not much night life, and the rain can be intense in the winter months. Good camping is available. The motels and pubs have some decent accommodations, but camping is really the way to go. There are some incredibly beautiful beaches here, with good surf, close to the camping areas. Most of the spots are easily accessible, it has all the comforts of

home, the surf is good, the people friendly. What are you waiting for?

Victoria: The land made famous by Bell's Beach, *"The Endless Summer"* and the legend of Wayne Lynch. Victoria is a rugged state, with big surf, and lots of it. It gets wet and cold. There are lots of places to explore, and big, sometimes heavy cold-water surf spots can be found. Prepare for rain.

Western Australia: Have a good car, plenty of tools and lots of water, if you plan on driving across the Nullabor Plain to Western Australia. Also, bring a bigger board if you plan on riding the heavier waves that break there. The surf can go to 15 feet. In general, it breaks hard.

The train is an option, and the *Indian-Pacific Line* sells a fourth class ticket kindly referred to as "The Supper Sitter." The train moves for four days in a straight line.

There are no accommodations for sleeping, except your seat. Those who are quick will jump into the dining car once it closes, and sleep on the couches there. Not the most comfortable way to travel, but you will meet some interesting characters, like the Aussie girl, Susie, (not her real name) who wanted to move to Nashville and become a country singer. She had a different country-western outfit on (including matching boots, belt, scarf, and hat) each day. At the start of each morning she had a very shy, introverted manner. By midday, she had usually pounded a few beers and was talkative. By evening, she had downed numerous beers, and the concerts began. You haven't lived until you've heard Patsy Cline with an Aussie accent.

Coming into Perth from the desert is really quite a site. Suddenly, there's this city of a million people in the middle of all this desert. The city has everything, including cars for rent and sale. Everything is a bit more dear on the west coast, however, and you might regret not having bought a car in Sydney. The residents are friendly, except for a few fiercely localistic types, usually from the U.S.

I'm sure I was not the first to charge down to Trigg Beach, thinking that I was going to find the ultimate Western Aussie wall of water, only to be greeted by onshore, two-foot mush, with 50 surfers out. Perth misses most of the good swells that hit Western Australia. To really get hooked into them, you need only to head north, where the land gets dry, and the ocean goes wild, south to the Margaret River region, or out into the islands. Regardless, you can't lose. The waves tend to be powerful and big, especially in the Australian winter season. Down south can be cold and rainy. A good wetsuit isn't a bad idea. The further north you go, however, the warmer the air and the water. Once you get more than 500 miles north of Perth, things get quite wild. Wedge-tailed eagles, red kangaroos, and cockatoos are plentiful. So are fish, and big, hungry sharks. There are no medical facilities anywhere near the major surfing areas, so bring a good first-aid kit, and be careful. Cuts can go bad quickly in the dry desert. Keep wounds clean, and bandaged.

There are local surfers in some of the areas, and for obvious reasons, they tend to be a bit territorial. Many have moved here from the major population centers, and are not interested in exposing the area. If you have a camera, be discreet. If you take some publishable photos, you don't have to name the spot, or even the region. It's a good rule of survival, just in case you want to go back again.

New South Wales: Nearly 750 miles of mostly surfable coastline. Average water temperatures in the high '60s. Air temp rarely drops below 70 F by day.

Surf, moderate, some excellent point and rock reef waves, rivermouths, and beach breaks. Some beautiful countryside, but quickly turning into one big Miami Beach. Sharks happen. Most rainfall-December to March.

Take your time getting to the Gold Coast. I know that you want to surf Kirra, but remember, so does everybody else. The wave is perfect when it's on, but very often packed. There are other spots, and you might just find one of them. The people are generally friendly, except for some of the surfers which can be territorial at times. Be cool. Sadly, some of the towns have gone out of the fish and chip and meat pie business, and have the pretentious sign "Bistro" offering a faux Euro feeling rather than a dinky-die genuine pass the piss and tomato sauce Aussie one. Pl-lease!

Queensland: The place where old aerobics instructors, and former pro surfers come to die. It's a hotdoggers paradise. The points fire some of the time, the night life rages all of the time. There are good rates in the pubs. Some youth hostels and camping. Find a board that works well in fast, down- the- line surf. Get a good rashguard, a spring suit, a gallon of sunscreen and a good hat. There are numerous surf shops for new boards, repairs, and other accessories. Everything is more expensive than in the U.S., so bring what you can.

Queensland, specifically the Gold Coast, is a year-round spring break. It's fast, expensive, fun, sunny, and filled with excellent surf and surfers. A go out at Kirra is a must, but don't expect to get too many waves to yourself. Burleigh is also a great wave, and there are numerous others in the area. The points fire in cyclone season, which ranges from December to as late as May. Other than that, you can get skunked, and end up surfing with 300 of your best friends at the Gold Coast reservoir known as Duranbah.

MEDICAL CARE: Excellent medical care provided in the main cities. Most of the small towns are also better than adequate. Have good insurance and plan to pay up front for treatment.

NATURAL HAZARDS: Big sharks in some of the more remote, unnetted regions. Some poisonous snakes and spiders on land. In the far north there are sea snakes.

UNNATURAL HAZARDS: Don't surf the city beaches after a hard rain. The water will be absolutely filthy. Oh, and don't shoot your mouth off about how great your country is when the local rugby team is taking over the town watering hole.

FURTHER ON: There are waves to the north of the Gold Coast, and some even to the north of Noosa Heads, beyond the Great Barrier Reef. Airfare is quite cheap to New Guinea, Indonesia, Fiji and New Zealand.

NEW ZEALAND

FIRST GLIMPSE: *Once again, Hynson and August. This time at a long left called Ragland in the original "Endless Summer."*

In 1973 I rented a house with a New Zealand surfer named Jim Carney, on the beach in Gisborne. The entire three-bedroom unit went for $18 a week, and my share was $6. I worked part-time in a Mauri pub making about $40 a week, and was able to save most of it. Beer in the pub was seven cents a glass. The best milk I have ever tasted was four cents a pint, abalone fritters could be purchaed from street vendors for ten cents. Fruit and vegetables were nearly free. Cars and petrol were outrageous, but we never wanted to go anywhere. Everything except the bad, expensive cars has changed.

The only localistic vibes I encountered in my entire six months in the country were from two brothers who had moved to a remote point from, you guessed it, Southern California.

Once when helping a young New Zealand school child to do a report on the environment, I suggested the obvious, find a place that has been ruined, and take a photo of it. The kid agreed to that, and we unsuccessfully spent the next two days trying to find a place that had been ruined.

I have heard recently that the ozone has become extremely thin over New Zealand, and that excessive amounts of sun block are necessary if you plan on surfing in mid-day. There is camping, but youth hostels are the way to go.

BEST SEASON FOR SURF: Good surf can be found in all seasons. The best weather, however, is from November through February.

SURFBOARDS: Something for moderate surf. The board you ride most often in Southern California would do nicely. A longboard is good for some spots.

OTHER SURF ACCESSORIES: A spring suit in summer. Fullsuit and booties in winter. In the winter on the South Island surfers have been known to wear fullsuit, gloves, booties, hood and Vasoline on the the exposed parts of the face. There are some well-supplied surf shops, but prices can be higher than in the U.S.

WEATHER: New Zealand summers are generally moderate, but the winters are usually very cold and wet. Bring something to keep the rain off.

CROWDS: Only at the main spots.

AIR TRANSPORTATION: Entry to New Zealand is generally by air, and usually into Aukland and less often in Wellington or Christchurch, on the South Island.

Cheap Flights: Can be inexpensive when used as a stopover to or from Australia. Ask your travel agent. Check the Sunday "travel section" of the newspaper.

DOCUMENTS: Passports are required for all visitors and must be valid for at least three months beyond the date the visitor plans on leaving the country. Work visas are required for those visitors intending to work.

U.S. students may work in New Zealand between April 1 and October 31 if they are considered eligible. Apply to: *CIEE Work Abroad*, 205 E. 42nd St., New York, NY 10017. Phone: (212) 661-1414. Other work visas require a recent passport photo, valid passport, evidence of onward travel, a written job offer from a prospective New Zealand employer, a police clearance. there is a $90 fee for applicants of some countries. Contact the New Zealand Consulate General: (310) 207-1605 for further information.

GROUND TRANSPORTATION: Driving is on the left hand side of the road. A traveller being this far from home, it's not a bad idea to have an International Driver's License. Still, visitors from the U.S., Australia, Great Britan, South Africa and some other countries can use licenses from home. If you're from Southern California you might be suprised to find farmers driving sheep across the roads. The sheep have the right of way.

Buses and trains operate throughout the country, but aren't much good for those who are on a surf safari. Trains and buses will take surfboards, but make sure that they are well protected. The ferry connects north and south islands. The roads are good, but transportation is difficult in New Zealand, unless you can afford a good rent-a-car and $2.50 per gallon for petrol. All of the major car rental companies—Avis, Hertz, Budget etc. are easy to find in the cities. Cars are expensive any way you look at it—about $125-$150 per day for a Toyota Corolla or a Mitsubishi Mirage. Mid-sized cars run about $150-$190 per day. Independent car rentals sometimes offer a better deal.

Basic campervans, or what Americans call RVs can be rented, starting at about $100 per day in the low season. There are numerous places around the country that rent campervans.

For those on a budget, and who isn't, there are opportunities to buy cars and resell them. The best places for this are in Auckland or Wellington. Check the bulletin boards at the local youth hostels for the best deals.

Tip: Don't be fooled by the price of $1.00 per. This stands for liters. Petrol runs about $2.50 per U.S. gallon.

Cars can be purchased on the "buy back system" from some dealers. This means just what it says, and while you don't have to sell the car back to the dealer, they are obliged to buy it back, and will pay about half of what you bought it for. Places offering the "buy back system" include:

Clarkes: (in Auckland). Phone: 52 02 003
Wheel's: (in Christchurch). Phone: 03 366 48 55

Buying a car might just be the best way to go in New Zealand. Cars are very expensive, however. The best, cheapest places to buy used cars are through the major newspapers, the auctions or the car fairs. Expect to pay between $1,500 to $4,500 for a beater. A decent vehicle will run about $8,000 and up. Roads are good, but there are a few radical conditions to negotiate. Driving is on left side of the road.

Auctions: *New Market Car Fair*
Saturday mornings: 09 524 9183

Hammer Auctions
Phone: 09 579 2344
Call for times and location.

North Shore Car Fair
Saturdays, call for location
Phone: 09 480 5612

Hitchhiking is legal and relatively easy in New Zealand, and the person offering a ride may even invite you to stay a few days in this friendly country. Don't stick out your thumb, but point your finger toward the road.

Tip: Get there before the camera crews for the America's Cup film everything in sight, and attract too many tourists.

CURRENCY EXCHANGE: One U.S. dollar = 1.40 New Zealand dollars. *Exchange rates will fluctuate.*

CURRENT: 230V, 50 cycles AC

LODGING: Bed and breakfasts are good and fairly inexpensive, motor inns are a good deal, and sometimes locals will ask you to share the rent if you're going to be around for a while. Still, the best bet for those passing through are one of the over 50 youth hostels. The following hostels are the ones located near the ocean. Credit Card Booking Number: Phone: 09 379 4224. Bring a sleeping bag. Hostels are open only to members of the *Youth Hostel Federation.* Apply for membership in Los Angeles by writing the Los Angeles Council, 1502 Palos Verdes Dr. N., Harbor City, CA 90710. You can also buy membership within New Zealand.

Akaroa
Akaroa Associate Hostel, Mt Vernon Lodge
Rue Balguerie, P.O. Box 51, Akaroa
Phone: (3) 304-7180 - $13

Auckland
Auckland City Hostel, Corner City Rd & Liverpool St,
Auckland
Phone: (9) 309-2802 Fax: (9) 373-5083 - $19

Christchurch
Cora Winding Hostel
9 Eveleyn Couzins Ave, Richmond, Christchurch
Phone: (3) 389-9199 - $14

Cormandel
Tidewater Tourist Park Associate Hostel
270 Tiki Rd, Coromandel
Phone: (7) 866-8888 - $13

Dargaville
The Greenhouse Hostel
13 Portland Street, Dargaville
Phone: (9) 439-6342 - $12

Dunedin
Strafford Gables Youth Hostel
71 Stafford St., Dunedin
Phone: (3) 474-1919 - $14

Gisborne
Gisborne Youth Hostel
32 Harris St, Gisborne
Phone: (6) 867-3269 - $14

Great Barrier Island
Typhena Associate Hostel
Pohutukawa Lodge
Post Office, Tryphena, Great Barrier Island
Phone: (9) 429-0211 - $13

Greymouth
Kainga Hostel
15 Alexander St, Gerymouth
Phone: (3) 768-4951 - $13

Kaikoura
Maui Youth Hostel
Esplanade, Kaikoura
Phone: (3) 319-5931 - $14

Kaitaia
Kaitaia Youth Hostel
160 Commerce St, Kaitaia
Phone: (9) 408-1840

Kerikeri
Kerikeri Youth Hostel
Main Rd, Kerikeri
Phone: (9) 407-9391

Napier
Napier Youth Hostel
277 Marine Pde, Napier
Phone: (6) 835-7039 - $14

Nelson
Nelson Youth Hostel
42 Weka St, Nelson
Phone: (3) 548-8817 - $14

New Plymouth
Rotary Lodge Associate Hostel
Willow Grove, 12 Clawton St, New Plymouth
Phone: (6) 753-5720 - $13

Oamaru
Red Kettle Seasonal Hostel, 2 Reed St, Oamaru
Phone: (3) 434-5008 - $13

Opoutere
Opoutere Youth Hostel
via Waihi, Opoutere, Whangamata
Phone: (7) 865-9072 - $14

Pigeon Bay
Kukupa Seaonal Associate Hostel
Pettigrews Rd
Pigion Bay, Banks Peninsula
Phone: (3) 304-6888 - $9

Russell
Russell Associate Hostel, Orongo Bay Motor Camp
Whakapara Rd, Oronog Bay, Russell
Bay of Islands.
Phone: (9) 403-7704 - $12

Takaka
Takaka Summer Hostel
Golden Bay High School
Meihana Street, Takaka
Phone: (3) 525-9067 - $12

Waiheke Island
Onetangi Youth Hostel
Seaview Road, Onetangi
Waiheke Island
Phone: (9) 372-8971 - $14

Whangarei
Whangarei Youth Hostel
52 Punga Grove Avenue, Whangarei
Phone: (9) 438-8954 - $13

FOOD: Fresh fruits and vegetables as well as all types
of meat are available throughout the country. The food
is good, and there is nothing out of the ordinary to watch

for at any of eating establishments. Sometimes, however, the preparation of food in restaurants can be unimaginative. There is no tipping at the restaurants.

WATER: A lot of places still use rain water, which is about the safest, cleanest and best tasting that you can get anywhere.

PHONES: Country code: (64). Main cities and area codes: Auckland (9), Christchurch (3), Dunedin (3), Rotorua (7), Wellington (4).

MEDICAL CARE: It's a clean country for the most part, so nothing really unhealthy about it. Where once health services were nearly free for visitors, this is no longer the case, and insurance is recommended. Good hospitals in the main cities, and good to adequate in most small towns.

NATURAL HAZARDS: I have personally witnessed sharks in some regions of the North Island. Other than that, there are no real water hazards.

UNNATURAL HAZARDS: Normal precautions in some parts of the big cities, and don't offend the Mauris.

FURTHER ON: While New Zealand has its share of good surf, the harsh winters eventually drive surfers to Australia, where there is better weather, more opportunity to find work in the surf industry and generally better surf. If you are looking for surf paradise, don't count on New Zealand. If, on the other hand, it's peace and quiet, decent surf, friendly people and green hills that you're looking for, this could be the place for you.

FIJI

FIRST GLIMPSE: *We had heard of Fiji and even seen some small waves, but it wasn't until those first shots of "Restaurants" on Tavarua, that it became a world-class destination.*

BEST SEASON FOR SURF: March through September, but the swell, which stomps in from the south compliments of The Roaring 40s, can bring waves of size at any time. A recent "New Zealander" which hit the West Coast of the U.S. at about 4 to 6 feet was reportedly 15 feet at Cloudbreak.

    The Sigatoka River mouth at Club Masa is about the only sand-bottomed break on the island. Otherwise, expect mostly long paddles, up to 30 minutes, out to some fast, hollow surf. A lot of the boat captains in the harbors know where the surf is, and will take you out there for a fee. Of course there's always Tavarua. $125.00 per day.

SURFBOARDS: A big board is not out of the question, as the surf can often top 12 feet. Mostly, however, you're looking at barrels of fun in Rocky Point-like conditions at 4 to 6 feet. Bring at least two boards, if you can. Bring something a little longer for places like Cloudbreak, in case it gets big. While the pros can handle boards out there in the mid-7-foot range, be realistic about your own size (most of them aren't very big) and your ability (most of them surf better than you do) and adjust accordingly.

OTHER SURF ACCESSORIES: Thin spring suits provide extra protection against the sun and the coral. Some like vests for morning and evening sessions. Thin booties are advisable. Bring at least two thick leashes, a stack of tropical wax, and a rashguard (preferably long sleeved), mosquito repellent, net and coils.

WEATHER: Hot and humid. Rains a lot, but most islands have a dry side. Even in the coolest months, May through December, the temperature doesn't drop below 65. Driest months:June through September. Wind conditions are generally favorable for surfing.

CLOTHING: Dress casually, and conservatively. Wear shirts with sleeves. Skimpy clothing is frowned upon, and should never be worn in the remote villages. Bring slaps, hat and sunglasses.

Sun protection: Bring a hat, and plenty of sunscreen with an SPF factor of at least 15.

Tip: Electronic and photographic equipment can be a bargain at the duty-free shops. Don't be afraid to haggle over the price.

AIR TRANSPORTATION: Check the Sunday newspapers "travel section." Check the "General Information" section of this book under "Air Transportation." While its own destination, Fiji can also be a stop along the way to places like Australia and New Zealand, Hawaii and South America. Try to book it as a stop-over.

Carriers include: *Air New Zealand, Qantas, Air Pacific, Japan Airlines, Canadian Airlines, International Polynesian Airlines,* and *Air Nauru.*

DOCUMENTS: You'll need a valid passport, and proof of either round-trip ticket or onward passage. Visa issued for 30 days upon arrival and can be extended to six months.

Embassy: 2233 Wisconsin Ave,
N.W. #240 Washington D.C. 20007
Phone: (202) 337-8320

GROUND TRANSPORTATION:

Car rentals. All of the majors are here in force at Nadi International Airport, as well as some you may not have heard of. Expect to pay about U.S. $70 per day for a decent car. You'll need a valid driver's license from your own country. And, just to make it interesting, driving is done on the left-hand side of the road. Not a lot of gas stations around. If you run out of gas near a small village, ask around, someone may have a bit of petrol. Roads are decent, with only occasional obstacles like chickens and cows in the way. Look out for pedestrians. The locals can also be a little erratic behind the wheel.

Avis: 722-233
Budget: 722-735
Central: 722-771
Hertz: 722-146
Khans: 723-506
Letz 722-803
National 722-267
Roxy: 722-763
Satellite: 722-219
Skyline: 723-980
Thrifty: 722-935
UTC: 722-811

Buses: Good transportation and good value.

Taxis: A good, inexpensive way to travel in Fiji. Bring soft racks. It's a good idea to negotiate a fare before getting inside.

The out-of-town traffic is mellow and a bicycle

might just be the ticket. If you don't plan on leaving the main island of Viti Levu, hook up your *Wheelie,* and head out on the highway. Bring a good lock, and park your bike where you can see it. Hitchhiking is fairly easy for the foreigner.

LANGUAGE: English is widely spoken on Fiji, but if you are interested in learning some Fijian phrases and impressing the islanders, try Albert Schultz's *"Say it in Fijian"* (University Press of Honolulu, Hawaii 1979). As with all cultures that you visit, you will pick up some enjoyable phrases along the way.

CURRENCY EXCHANGE: One U.S. dollar = 1.29 Fiji dollars. Exchange rates will fluctuate.

ELECTRICAL CURRENT: Mostly 220 V, 50 cycles AC throughout Fiji. Most hotels will have, 110 converters. Adapters can be brought from home or purchased at duty-free shops or electrical supply stores in Fiji.

LODGING:
Camping: Don't set up a camp site unless you are given permission. Some camping is permitted at the *Ovalau Holiday Resort* and the *Seashell Cove Resort.* For permission to camp in other areas, contact: *The Lands and Survey Section of The Ministry of Lands.* Phone: 211 516 in Suva. If you have any doubts, ask landowner.

Visitors can sometimes score a place in one of the **Government Guest Houses.** Check with local district offices. Rooms are available for about $ 5 per night.
Hotels can go from about $25 up to about $110.
Youth Hostel Association members are entitled to dis-

counts in Fiji. The following have YHA approval, and range from Fiji $ 5 - $ 13 a night. Some of the other backpackers places around town can be sketchy.

YHA Youth Hostels:
Hideaway Resort
Queen's Road, Coral Coast
P.O. Box 233, Sigatoka, Fiji
(20 km east of Sigatoka)
Phone: (679) 500-177
Fax: (679) 520-025

Nadi Bay Motel
Wailoaloa Beach Rd
Private Mail Bag NAP0359
Nadi, Fiji:
(midway between Nadi Airport and township).
Phone: (679) 723-599
Fax: (679) 790-092

Seashell Cove Resort Momi Bay
P.O. Box 9530, Nadi, Fiji (37 km south of Nadi)
Phone: (679) 790-100/393
Fax: (679) 790-294
Courtesy car available through Nadi airport by arrangement.
There are some backpacker-type places around. *The Traveler's Beach Resort* in Nadi is about $12 a night.

FOOD: Be careful of some restaurants, and be sure that water and ice are from a clean source before partaking. There is a wide variety of food in Fiji. Indian food is popular, healthy, and delicious. Fresh fruits purchased from the local markets should be washed and peeled. There are moderately priced Indonesian, Indian, Chinese and Japanese foods available.
If offered kava, do try some. *E dua na bilo?* (Try a

cup?) is the invitation. The muddy looking liquid is extracted from a root in the pepper family. It leaves a slight numbness in the tongue, and may be considered a mild stimulant. The better effect of drinking kava, however, is the one achieved by the bonding of you with your hosts.

PHONES: Country code: (679). 17 hours ahead of Eastern Standard time. Everything above (except presumably the time) is subject to change.

MEDICAL CARE: While tropical, Fiji is free from many of the really rugged tropical diseases like malaria. Water is relatively safe in most cities. Health requirements change. Check your tourist bureau.

Immunizations for cholera and yellow fever are required, if you are coming from an infected area. You may also need tetanus, typhoid and infectious hepatitis shots.

Water is almost always potable, but if you are unsure, drink bottled water or soft drinks. Avoid gathering seafood in the lagoons near population centers, wash vegetables, and peel any fruit yourself. You still might get the runs, just because you are not used to the local food.

Lice and bed bugs can be a problem in some areas. Check the hotel mattress. If you see blood spots on the bedding, keep moving.

STDs: Take the usual precautions.

Medical attention can be horrifying to decent. If you have a major emergency, call your embassy for the best place to go. Decent clinics and doctors are available in the main towns. For major emergencies, a flight to Sydney is probably your best bet. Have good insurance. Pharmacies throughout island.

By the late 1980s Tavarua had become a major surf destination. And no wonder; just look at the place. It may be a long ways to go just to go left, but what a left!

But Tavarua is not the only place to surf in Fiji. There are heaps of other places, maybe not as good, but well worth the trip. There are, however, very few breaks that do not require a boat to get to. Reef passes are the norm here. And with over 300 islands, many of them uninhabited, you can find your own spot. One word of caution, however. Sailing in these waters is difficult at best, and boats and lives are lost on a regular basis. If you get in trouble out here, you're a long way from a hospital or anything that we consider civilized.

The **people** are extremely friendly and tolerant, as is evidenced by the fact that three of the world's major religions, Christianity, Hinduism, and Islam all exist in harmony.

Water temperature: Never drops below 70 F.

Tavarua Resort
Considered by many to be the ultimate surf vacation. Contact: Tavarua Island Tours Inc. Phone: (805)686-4551. Fax: (805) 683-6696.

Good gifts for the friendly Fijians are inexpensive toys for the children, guitar strings, and T-shirts.

Cameras and film are available at good prices in Suva.

NATURAL HAZARDS: Coral snakes, sea snakes, sharks.

FURTHER ON: Nadi International Airport goes everywhere you want to be. Ask your travel agent about *"Circle Pacific"* and *"Round the World Tickets."* If you're on your way to someplace like Australia, you might get Fiji thrown in for an extra $50 or so. There are inexpensive boat trips to outer islands.

Brewer

BALI

FIRST GLIMPSE: *We sat huddled one windy evening in 1973 in the Byron Bay Pub, watching Alby Falzon's then-new surf movie "Morning Of the Earth." There, on the screen were all the Australian breaks I had recently ridden and learned to love, in a 90-minute package. Also contained in that package was a surprise, at a place that I had never heard connected with surfing until then—Bali. Rusty Miller and Steven Cooney took on solid 10-foot Uluwatu alone. We were spellbound, so much so that within a decade the world was off to Indonesia to discover places like G'land, and Periscopes.*

Keep in mind that Bali is just across the street from Australia, and that the place couldn't remain unsurfed for long. What was once the secret of Indonesia is now merely the landing dock to paradise. Still, there is plenty to see and do, and many great waves to be had in Bali itself.

Just last year a friend of mine said "Every day in Bali is the best day of your life." I think that it's still true.

BEST SEASON FOR SURF: Surf can vary from big and powerful, to fun and playful. Winds are variable according to the seasons, and swell is consistent all year long. Biggest waves, however, usually arrive between June and September, which is winter in the Southern Hemisphere. (Keep in mind that the seasons in the Southern Hemisphere are exactly the opposite of those in the Northern Hemisphere, and that the further north you go, the warmer it gets. The further south you go, the colder it gets. (Going north for the winter seems odd at first.)

SURFBOARDS: Mid-7 foot boards with a little extra weight for the offshore winds seem to work in most everything, but just about everything works. You shouldn't need much over an 8' 0" for any conditions. A longboard is a nice touch for the smaller days.

OTHER SURF ACCESSORIES: No wetsuits are needed, but sadistic surfers who enjoy pulling into barrels that they might not make, wear spring suits as protection against shallow reefs. A good rashguard (preferably one with long sleeves) is essential. Bring thin booties for the reefs. A vest for mornings and evenings is nice. Lots of tropical wax. At least one extra-durable leash. Goggles can help with the glare (try "Spex"). Bring a waterproof hat, such as those from *"Made In The Shade."* Sunscreen with an SPF of 15 or over. Instant ding-repair kit. Most surf accessories as well as ding repairs can be found in Kuta.

Tip: According to world traveler and ASP pro surfer Jim Hogan, the book *"Indo Surf and Lingo"* by Peter Neely is "not good, it's awesome." The book tells you when and where to score the best surf.

WEATHER: Bali is hot and humid much of the year, but cooler and drier between April and December. Big crowds of surfers come in from Australia during their holidays—Easter, Christmas.

AIR TRANSPORTATION:
Arrival: Jakarta or Denpasar. *Garuda* is the national airline. Call them for reservations out of Los Angeles at: (213) 387-0149. Low season is from early January through late May, and early September through mid December. High season: June, August, and late December. Reconfirm flights 72 hours in advance when arriving or leaving Bali.

Cheap flights: Check the student discounts and Sunday newspapaper "travel sections." Ask your travel agent, you might be able to get Bali as a stop-over to another destination. Check the "General Information" section of this book under "Air Transportation."

DOCUMENTS: Passport and onward/return ticket. Visa not required for tourist/business stay of up to two months (non-extendable). If you hope to stay longer, contact *Embassy of the Republic of Indonesia*, 2020 Mass. Ave., N.W., Washington, D.C. 20036. (202) 775-5200 or nearest consulate: California: (213) 383-5126. Hawaii: (808) 524-4300. New York: (212) 879-0600. All document requirements are subject to change, so check with your travel agent or consulate for latest information.

GROUND TRANSPORTATION: Buses, bemos, taxis and rental cars: Bemos are mini-buses or small pick-up trucks with two rows of seats. Bemo drivers are famous for overcharging tourists. A general rule is, if they charge you 500 rp, offer them 300. If they laugh and shrug it off, you know that they've overcharged you. If they make a scene, the fare was probably correct. Beware of pick-pockets on buses and bemos. Taxis are generally a decent deal. Use the official taxi counter and pay for your ride in advance. Bring soft surf racks. Check the meters before you get in, and agree upon the fare before leaving for your destination.

The major national rent-a-car places are all highly visible. They are, however, quite expensive. Local car rental can be cheaper. Popular vehicles are the *Suzuki Jinny* and the *Volkswagen Safari*. One problem with the *VW Safari* or any soft-top convertible, is that you can't lock up your valuables. If you rent a car, check it out thoroughly. Petrol is reasonably priced.

Kuta is the cheapest place to rent a car.

Tip: Try desperately to avoid accidents. If you get into a minor prang, it might be best to settle things at the side of the road. If there is major injury or death involved, be very careful. Try to get the police on the scene as soon as possible, and send someone that you know and trust to contact the consulate. You might get your vehicle impounded and spend a few nights in jail until the matter is resolved. If you are driving, make sure that you are experienced in rough roads, and are able to cope with chaotic traffic, and local authorities. Once you get into the countryside, there is little congestion.

Motorbikes are popular methods of transportion and can be rented in many places. Make sure, however, that your travel insurance (if you have such a thing) specifically covers motorbikes. An International Driver's License is required. The fine for driving without a license is 2,000,000 rp.

LANGUAGE: Bahasa Indonesian, Javanese. English and Dutch are most commonly spoken foreign languages.

Water temperatures never drop below 70 F.

Haggling: The set price is not always the price you have to pay. When buying art objects and other tourist items, feel free to haggle over the cost.

CURRENCY EXCHANGE: One U.S. dollar = 1,522 rupiah. Exchange rates will fluctuate.

ELECTRICAL CURRENT: 220V - 50-cycles, AC. Some small towns run on 110.

Tip: You may think that this is a pretty free place, but drugs of all sorts bring with them extreme penalties. You don't want to go to an Indonesian jail.

Tip: Some people have paid for their trips to Bali by purchasing and then selling some of the many inexpensive and well-made items found here. Bedspreads, clothing, jewelry—all have turned a profit. If you are thinking of starting your own import company, be aware that many have done the same thing, and the market may be saturated. Other than that, you'll find a lot of things to bring home for your own enjoyment.

LODGING:

Hostels: *Indonesian Youth Hostel Association*
Ggd PKON Kantor Menpora RI, J1 Gerbang Pemuda
No 3 Senaan, Jakarta, 10270, Indonesia
Phone: (21) 573-8156   Fax: (21) 573-8313
> Some hostles have self-catering facilities. There may be a small charge for use of kitchen utensils. Reservations are essential and should be made direct to the hostel. *The Kopo, Vagabond* and *Vogels* youth hostels offer 10 percent discounts to Hostelling International members.

Bali International Hostel
Jalan Mertrasari 19, Banjar Suwang Kangin
Sidakarya, Denpassar Selatan, Bali
Phone/fax: (361) 263-912
U.S. $ 6- U.S. $ 8
Pick-up offered for hostellers with reservations.

Bali- Panji Sakti
Panji Sakti,
Singaraja-Seririt St.,
P.O. Box 127
Code Pos 81101, Singaraja, Bali

Yogyakarta-Vogels
Vogels YH
APPI-Travellers Information Center, JI
Astamulya 76, Kaliurang, Yogyakarta
U.S. $3 - U.S. $5

Yogyakarta-Vagabond
Vagabond YH, J1 Prawirotaman MG III 589
(JL Sisingamangaraja 28B), Togyakarta
Central Java
Phone/Fax: (274) 71207
Open 24 hours
U.S. $3-U.S. $7.50

Other Lodging:
Adi Yasa Hotel
Phone: 222-679

Simon's Seaside Cottages
Phone: 41183

FOOD: The local food is delicious, but may take some getting used to. As with Mexican food in Mexico, the less you pay, the better the meal. Try to insure that plates are washed, and everything is sanitary. A great variety of fruits are available, many of which you have never heard of if you haven't been beyond an American supermarket. Bottled drinking water is readily available, as are beer and soft drinks.

PHONES: Country Code (62) City code, Despensar (361).

Emergencies: If you have problems that constitute an emergency, contact your embassy or consulate. They will give you medical referrals and legal advice. Serious medical problems should not be trusted to small-town doctors. Try to make it to the *Nusa Dua Hotel* complex. Better yet, try to get on a plane to Sydney, or home. Get medical insurance. If you need surgery, go to the more expensive hotels. Expect to pay cash, up front.

MEDICAL CARE: Be careful to see that needles are clean and sterilized. It might be a good idea to bring your own needles in a first-aid kit, and let a local doctor stitch you up. Coral cuts are common. Keep them clean.

Health watch: Try to avoid unwashed raw foods, and undercooked meats. Don't drink the tap water. Malaria suppressant is highly recommended. Innoculations against typhoid, cholera, tuberculosis, hepatitis, and dengue fever may be necessary. Health requirements change. For latest information contact: U.S. Chamber of Commerce: Citibank Bldg., 8th floor, Jakarta J1; Phone: (21) 332-602.

A certificate of vaccination against yellow fever is required by all people arriving from infected areas and for all persons arriving from countries in the endemic zones.

- **Cholera** is present in some areas of the country. Strict adherence to food and water precautions lowers risks.

- **Malaria** is present in rural areas. Large cities are risk free. Check Costa Rican section under the "Medical Care" entry for precautions against malaria.

- **Diarrhea** risks are high. Break into unfamiliar foods slowly. Drink bottled water or soda.

Avoid uncooked vegetables in restaurants. Peel
all fruit yourself. Be sure that pork, chicken and
fish are fresh and well cooked.

- **HIV** exists worldwide. Take normal precautions.

- **Insect-borne diseases:** Peak transmission season is March through April, at the end of the rainy season.

Tip: Wear slaps on beaches to avoid some parasites. Long sleeves and pants after dark. Avoid after-shaves or perfumes. Use mosquito repellent liberally and get into screened areas after dark.

- **Japanese Encephalitis** is a viral illness transmitted through infected mosquitoes. Risk highest in rainy season. Vaccine is available for travelers who plan on staying in rural areas over 30 days or for individuals who plan to visit high-risk agricultural regions, such as rice-growing or pig-farming areas. Insect precautions must also be observed.

- **Rabies**: Pre-exposure vaccination is recommended for those persons intending to stay for long and come in contact with animals.

- **Schistosomiasis** is a parasitic disease that has been reported in Indonesia. May be acquired during swimming, bathing, or accidental immersion in certain freshwater lakes, rivers and streams. Chlorinated and salt water are safe.

Recommended Immunizations: Update tetanus/diphtheria, measles/mumps/rubella, and polio vaccines as appropriate to age and date of last dose. Havrix (Covered in "General Information") and a typhoid fever vaccine are strongly recommended for all travelers.

Medical Facilities: The general level of sanitation and health is below U.S. standards. Emergency services are generally inadequate outside of major cities. Insurance may not be valid. Bring a good first-aid kit. Tweezers for sea urchin spines, and Betadine for your cuts are necessary. Keep cuts clean and watch for signs of staph. For more information on medical facilities contact the Centers for Disease Control's International Traveler's hotline at (404) 332-4559.

CRIME: Crimes such as passport theft occur mostly in high population areas. Guard valuables carefully, and report stolen passports to U.S. Embassy or nearest consulate. Beware of pick-pockets when in a crowd. Possession of drugs can lead to a 10-year sentence.

POSTAL SERVICE: Most towns will have a post office, open from 8 a.m. to 2 p.m. Mail should be sent with the last name underlined or in capital letters. Also write 'Kantor Pos', the name of the town and Bali, Indonesia. The Despensar Post Office is a hassle to get to, so you might want to consider having mail sent to Kuta, Ubud, Singaraja or a convenient post office near you.

A FEW USEFUL WORDS AND PHRASES:
yes: *ya*
no: *tidak*
good, well: *bagus, baik*

bad: *jeiek*
eat: *makan*
big: *besar*
small: *kecil*
water: *air*
welcome: *selamat datang*
good morning: *selamat pagi*
good afternoon: *selamat sore*
good night: *selamat malam*
please: *silakan*
thank you: *terima kasih*
sleep: *tidur*
room: *kamar*
bathroom: *kamar mandi*
toilet: *way say*
bus: *bis*
train: *kereta-api*
help: *disini*
shut up and surf: *just kidding.*

Tipping is not a general practice in Bali, but the major hotels will add a tip into the cost of meals.

Tip: It is best not to give money to beggars.

Tip: Even if the local surfer is a beginner, treat him with respect. Hey, it's their home.

Travel light and dress conservatively. In and around Kuta, the locals are used to tourists, but they will respect you more if you adhere to their customs. Shorts are frowned upon in country towns. Wear shirts with sleeves. Tank tops or anything that shows the shoulder is not considered respectable. Dress nicely, especially if you are visiting temples or government offices. When visiting temples, buy a temple scarf, or you can rent one at most of the temples. Show respect for the priests.

Don't stand above them, trying to take their pictures. Women are not allowed in the temples during their periods. Casual, clean and conservative is a good rule. Sandals are generally okay. Bathing suits are definitely out when traveling around town.

FURTHER ON: Charter yachts take groups of surfers around the island, or to G'land, Lombok or Sumbawa. The charters are advertised in surf press publications available throughout Kuta. Prices start at about U.S. $75 a day per person.

Nias is a difficult and expensive place to travel to. It has a high incident of malaria, is often crowded with kooks, and the surf is fickle. The journey begins in Medan, in northeast Sumatra. Once there, however, the surf can turn on, and accommodation is dirt cheap.

Grajagan: Visas are not required. Get an international motorcycle license and rent a motorcycle for about U.S. $5.00 a day, or if you are more safety conscious and want to save money, get onto the bemo.

Australia: It's just a puddle-jump to Australia from Bali. If you want to see the Northern Territories and take a car down the coast, start in Darwin, and buy a car. Expect to pay about U.S. $2,000 for a basic beater. Make sure that you have your visa and passports worked out before you land in Australia. If you want to get right into the surf, fly directly to Perth, Brisbane, or Sydney.

Bali is only the beginning, and with countless islands in the chain, Indonesia is an explorer's dream. Also, anything can happen in Indonesia. There are tigers, malaria, floods, droughts and tsunamis to contend with. Other than that, have a nice day!

Cassidy

TAHITI

FIRST GLIMPSE: *"Endless Summer"* with Mike Hynson and Robert August surfing "Ins and Outs." The second glimpse had a greater impact—a rough film from lifeguard Jim Lischer, in the late '70s showing powerful waves on outside reefs.

Gosh, the impact of Bruce Brown's "Endless Summer"! That Mid '60s visit to Tahiti was a charming milestone, and proved that there was indeed some surf on those islands. Still, it would take at least another decade, (probably because of the invention of the surf leash) before someone would paddle out and surf the reef passes. With so many epic surf shots coming from Tahiti, it seems absurd now that modern surfing there is only about 30 years old.

Check the photos—world class waves abound in clear, warm water. But make no mistake—most of the surf is for advanced surfers only. The hazards are many, but so are the rewards. Be friendly to the local Tahitians.

BEST SEASON FOR SURF: May-September. This, as good fortune would have it, is also the dry season. Surf is mostly on barrier reefs. Six to 10 feet, sometimes bigger. Powerful and hollow.

SURFBOARDS: Boards snap regularly. Bring a backup if you can afford it. Boards should range on the longer side—think surf from "Back Door" to "Second Reef Pipeline". Maybe not quite as heavy, but very thick and hollow. Some airlines can charge up to $40 per board, each way. On airlines such as *Air New Zealand* boards are usually free. Check around.

OTHER SURF ACCESSORIES: A rashguard for the sun is the only thing required. Some surfers prefer vests for early morning-late evening sessions. Wetsuits like spring suits are sometimes used for protection against coral cuts. Booties are a good idea. Bring at least two strong leashes. Lots of tropical wax.

Bring sun screen, hat, glasses, insect repellent, ding-repair kit. There is at least one surf shop that offers surf accessories and ding repair in Papeete.

WEATHER: Tropical, but moderate. High humidity. It can rain a lot in the wet season - November-April. Temperatures never much over 80 F or lower than 70 F. Seasons are reversed from those in the U.S., so winter is from June through September, and summer goes from December through February.

CROWDS: The local vibe, while generally good, can be a bit tough in places. Some of the local surfers are extremely good, especially considering the small talent pool they have to draw from.

Tip: Wait your turn, and don't let the locals think that you're French, even if you are. Shake hands with the locals in the lineup.

AIR TRANSPORTATION: Cheap flights through Circle Pacific, or an around-the- world ticket can be a good value here, if you plan on passing through Tahiti and going on to Australia or New Zealand. Student Travel. Check Sunday newspaper "travel sections." Arrival is through the Faaa International Airport, not far from Papeete. Many people arrive from Hawaii in Tahiti by yacht, and they sometimes need crews.
Islands in the Sun has some good package deals starting at around $900. Phone/fax: (310) 536-6266 .

DOCUMENTS: All of the travel documents required apply to all of French Polynesia, an island chain consisting of 130 islands. Of those, 14 islands are located in the Society Islands, and Tahiti is just one of those islands. Now that we've cleared that up, I guess it's safe to say that the place is totally bitchin'.

No visa required for a stay of up to one month. You need proof of round trip, or onward passage. For longer stays, call the French Embassy. Phone: (202) 944-6000. Requirements are subject to change. Check with embassy or your travel agent, before departure.

GROUND TRANSPORTATION: Le Truck is an inexpensive method of getting both you and your surfboard around the island. You can rent very small cars for about $30 a day. A motorcycle or a bicycle will work for some. A bicycle with a *Wheele* attached to carry your board and gear is not a bad idea, if you can find someplace to stash your stuff. Hitching is possible, but a surfboard makes it a lot harder. Bring soft racks.

LANGUAGE is Tahitian, but many people speak good English, or French.

CURRENCY EXCHANGE: One U.S. dollar = 87.07 French Pacific Francs (CFP). *Exchange rates will fluctuate.*

ELECTRIC CURRENT: 110 V, 60 cycles AC

LODGING: Places called "pensions," which are basic room and board can be rented from about $20 a day. At some hotels you can rent a "fare," which is something like a cabana. This is a cheap way to go. Some even have cooking facilities. Ask for a "residence guide" at travel agencies in Papeete.

Huahine:
Hotel Huahine.
Phone: 68-82-69
  About $22

Guynette's Pension
Phone68-83-75
About $30

Pension Enite
Phone: 68-82-37

Tahiti:
Hotel Le Legon. About $15, communal showers and bathrooms. For private shower and bathroom, add another $5. P.O. Box 634, Papeete. Don't expect any Gaugin originals in the rooms. Cleanliness, somewhere between Papillion and the Ritz.

Moorea:
Camping can be done on Moorea. Call: Moorea Camping: 56-14-47. Bring your own mosquito net. In Haapiti: Nelson and Josianne. Call: 56-15-18

Tip: Moorea has the most beautiful lagoon you've ever seen. Plan on diving it while you're there. Mask and snorkel can be rented at one of the hotels.

Motel Chez Albert
Phone: 56-12-76
$21

Raiat
Pension Marie-France
Phone: 66-37-10
Hostel with 5 rooms, 14 beds, toilet, 2 showers. Communal kitchen. Bunks are $13.50.

Raititea Village Hotel
Phone: 66-31-62
About $40 per night for a large fare which includes a kitchen.

Papeete
Motel Mahina Tea
Phone: 42-00-97.
About $27

Territorial Hostel Center
Phone: 42-88-50
Hostel Association members can stary for around $18. Doors close at midnight.

Of note: If you are taking the wife and kids, Tahiti can be a very expensive trip. If, however, you are going with the boys, it can be done for a lot less. Even so, the hotels can be bartered with, to a certain extent.

There is some camping, and it gets better as you get further from the main population centers. Still, make sure that you have permission from the landowner before pitching a tent. Offer money. Stay out of site of the main road, and guard your possessions well. Accommodation can be found in the low to mid-$20 range. Check The Tourist Board Office in Papeete for cheap places to stay. Phone: 429-626.

FOOD: No fast food, except in some parts of Papaeete. If you can find a place to get a hamburger, fries and a coke, expect to pay $15-$20. Stores close from 12 p.m. to 2 p.m. daily, and are not open on Sunday. Look for locally produced items, since everything imported has 100 percent duty attached to it. Make sure that any fish or meat you buy is fresh. Local fishermen will display their catch, and sell a whole fish, which can cost up to $100. Pack your own snacks-oatmeal, canned tuna, energy bars, etc., from home, if you've got the room. Mostly expensive, mostly good French restaurants, and a wide variety of other foods. Coconuts are plentiful and nutritious.

WATER: Water is generally considered drinkable, but you might not find it to your liking. Bottled water is the way to go.

PHONES: International Code (011). Country code: (689) plus local number. The local currency, especially the coins, can be difficult to work out on the pay phone. The best method is to buy a phone card from the local post office.

MEDICAL CARE: Health requirements are subject to change. Call tourist offices: Los Angeles: (213) 207-1919; Papeete, Tahiti: 429-626 or contact the French Government Tourist Office: (212) 757-1125. There is no malaria on Tahiti, but a mosquito net should be included in your travel kit. Keep cuts clean to avoid staph infection.

Be careful of some fresh fish. Chiguatera, a disease of tropical fish, exists. It can be extremely unpleasant. If diarrhea and a tingling around the mouth and limbs are present at the same time, you need to get to a doctor.

POSTAL: Post Restante (general delivery) at the post office. Mail can also be received at *American Express Office*.

NATURAL HAZARDS: On land, you need to be aware that coconuts can fall on you. They travel a long way, and they are very heavy. Coconuts can be purchased throughout Tahiti and some people will like the milk and the meat very much. However, don't try to climb the trees. They are a lot taller than they look. A fall from the top could be fatal.

The only beach breaks are on the island of Tahiti. The best surf in the Society Islands is on the reef passes. The waves are fast, hollow and powerful, and require that you are in good paddling shape. Boats can be rented through some of the hotels for a few hundred dollars. Try to split the cost about six ways. It's the only way to go, if you plan on staying out there a while. Otherwise, you'll need to paddle a long way. Practice paddling before you go, because the paddle takes between 20 and 45 minutes, and is longer on the way in because you're moving against the offshore wind and the current. Also, you'll be tired from surfing.

Most of the local Tahitians are in great shape from paddling canoes, and paddling out to the reef passes. There are many good surfers in the Society Islands these days, and a small group on Huahine can make you feel unwanted. Give them their space. They are a hearty bunch and they have learned to surf, not as most of us did, by being pushed near the sand in the whitewater on tiny days, but by paddling out to the reefs, taking off, and eating it!

You will see reef sharks on the inside reefs. Nobody seems to worry much about them. However, don't mess with them; treat them with all of the respect that you would a pit bull. The big sharks are on the outside reefs. On big days, or when the tide is going out, there is a real danger of being swept out to sea, beyond the reef. The rip in the middle of the pass can run like a river, and you don't want to be in it when it does. You don't want to lose your board. Any cord should be thick and reliable. If you do lose your board, play the edge of the wave to swim in. Avoid the impact zone, but don't head for the channel. You don't want to go in over the reef, but even that is preferable to getting swept out to sea. One local surfer reports that he could not get in over the reef on one very big day, and had to go over the falls and over the barrier reef in order to get back to shore.

Don't surf alone! You're about 30 minutes from the beach, and if you get hurt, you could be in real trouble. If you get cut, get out of the water. The sharks react to the scent of blood.

NATURAL HAZARDS: Sharp reefs, sea urchins, occasional stone fish, sharks.

UNNATURAL HAZARDS: Petty theft.

Tip: The main market in Papaette is worth a visit, to buy items you might want to bring back home.

Tip: The local people are reserved, and wary of outsiders. If you smile and wave at them, they'll generally return the greeting.

Caution: Beware of trying to sell your boards on the island. Boards are checked on the way into Tahiti, and on the way out. Keep even broken boards, because they are trying to discourage you selling your board on the island. If you are caught without the same number of boards you brought in, you will be forced to pay a large amount of duty.

FURTHER ON: Transportation to other islands can be accomplished by copra boat, ferry or plane. Most islands have airports, and are serviced by *Air Tahiti.* **Ferrys** are an inexpensive, unreliable way to travel from island to island. While schedules are available through the government tourist office, these are only approximations. This is a bad idea if you get seasick or are in a hurry. Getting a cabin costs about twice as much as doing without one, but can make a bad trip a lot easier. Purchase tickets at least a half day in advance. If you absolutely must be some place, camp out at the docks. Bring your own food if the captain allows it.

Taking a ferry or copra boat can be rough, especially to distant islands like Huahine, and especially during a storm. If you plan on visiting a lot of the islands, money can be saved by buying a pass for all islands.

Brewer

SOUTH AFRICA

FIRST GLIMPSE: *"The Endless Summer," watching Cape Saint Francis, with dropped jaw, like everybody else. Heartbreak of the decade: Finding out that the place that symbolized the dream for all of us has been ruined by development.*

Tip: Get out into the world before the developers pave it.

BEST SEASON FOR BEST SURF: May-July

SURFBOARDS: Bring a board that handles long, fast point breaks, and hollow tubes. Not many lefts in the country, but an occasional left-breaking ledge reminiscent of Big Rock in La Jolla, California.

OTHER SURF ACCESSORIES: Wetsuits. The further south you go, the more protection you will need. A fullsuit is needed for winter. Some wear gloves and booties. There are well-supplied surf shops in all of the major towns.

WEATHER: Semi-arid. Subtropical in some places along the coast. Expect sunny days and cool nights. Wear what you'd wear in Central and Southern California.

AIR TRANSPORTATION: International airports are in Johannesburg, Durban, and Cape Town. Confirm your flight within 72 hours. It's a long way from the U.S. West Coast. Try to get a stop in Europe to break things up.

Cheap Flights: All flights to South Africa are expensive because it's not on the way to or from any major destination. Check Sunday "travel sections" of major newspapers, and refer to the "General Information" section of this book.

DOCUMENTS: Passport and visa required. Obtain visa in advance of arrival. A multiple-entry visa is good for one year if passport is valid during that time. You will need to show proof of onward or return passage, and a visa to your next destination. Check with your travel agent or consulate for changes.

GROUND TRANSPORTATION: Trains are relatively inexpensive, and operate regularly between cities and towns. There is a decent bus network also.

From the airport in Port Elizabeth, you can call *"Sunshine Transport"* at: 932-221 for transporation to Jeffrey's Bay. Call ahead of time.

A YHA Card entitles you to discounts at some restaurants, pharmacies, and even pubs. Also *Interpax Passenger Services* (Main Line Trains): 25 percent discount *Imperial Car Rental:* 10 percent discount on daily rates *Translux* (National Coach Line): 10 percent discount.

Driving is on the left hand side of the road. An International Drivers License is required. Highways and roads are excellent.

All the major car rental agencies are available. Cars start at about R70 per day. Try: *Rent-A-Wreck:* (011) 402-7043. or *Council Car Hire*: (011) 789-2327. There are rental cars available in all major airports, and at J-Bay.

Roads are basically good. Johanesburg is the best place to buy a car. Check the Thursday *"Star"* for cars. Expect to pay R 6000 and up. Try the Sunday car market. Call: (011) 643-1183. Make sure the car you buy has a "road worthy certificate."

LANGUAGE: English/Afrikaans/Zulu/Xhosa.

CURRENCY EXCHANGE: One U.S. dollar = 3.23 rand. *Exchange rates will fluctuate.*

ELECTRICAL CURRENT: 250 V

PHONES: International code: (019) Country code (27). Main city area codes: Johannesburg, (11), Pretoria, (12), Cape Town, (21) Durban, (31). Port Elizabeth, (41). Dial "0" when calling within South Africa.

LODGING:
Hostels:
Cape Town Abe Baily
11 Maynard Rd, Muizenburg - 7951, Cape Town
Phone: (21) 788-2301, 788-4283 Fax: (21) 216-937
R $18

Cape Town-Belvidere
Higgo Crescent, Higgovale 8001, Cape Town
Phone: (21) 231-316 Fax: (21) 242-909
R $27

Cape Town-Rolling Stones
94 Lower Main Rd., Observatory, Cape Town 7925
Phone: (21) 448-1124
R $20-R $25

Cape Town-Stans Halt
The Glen, Camps Bay, Cape Town 8001
Phone: (21) 438-9037, 438-1405 Fax: (21) 216-937
R $18

Cape Town-Zebra Crossing Traveller's Lodge
82 New Church St., Cape Town 8001
Phone/fax: (21) 221-1265
R $20

IYHF is currently in negotiations with organizations within South Africa to expand the hosteling network. The following are available as supplementary accommodations for the time being:

Cape Town - The Albergo
5 Beckham St., Cape Town 8000
Phone/fax: (21) 230-515
R $20- R $85

Cape Town - Hip Hop Traveller's Shop
(I've never been there, but feel compelled to check it out, just because of the name.)
11 Vesperdene Rd., Green Point 8001, Cape Town
Phone/fax: (21) 439-2104
R $20. 24-hour free pick-up service

Durban
Durban Beach Hostel
19 Smith Street, Durban 4001, Natal
Phone: (31) 324-945 Fax: (31) 324-551
R $12

Jeffrey's Bay
12 Jeffrey St., Jeffrey's Bay
6330, Eastern Cape
Phone: (423) 931-379
R $15

Knysna
Knysna Hostel, 42 Queen St.
Knysna 6570
Phone: (445) 22-554
R $22

Mossel Bay
Mossel Bay Backpackers
1 Marsh St., Mossel Bay 6500
Garden Route
Fax/Phone: (444) 913-182
R $22. Free pick up in and around Mossel Bay

Plettenberg Bay
The Albergo, 8 Church St., Plettenberg Bay
Phone: (4457) 34434 Fax:(21) 230515
R $25. Shuttle service available

Port Elizabeth
Port Elizabeth Hostel
7 Prospect Hill Rd, Central,
Port Elizabeth 6000
Phone: (41) 560-697 Fax: (441) 746-054
R $22

Other Lodging
        According to La Jolla surfer and world traveler Henry Hunt, one of the best places to stay near Jeffrey's Bay is Mike Tabling's studio. The studio rents for less than 20 American dollars a night, and is located right at the kickout point of one of the best waves in the world. Phone: 011- 27421 961911 in order to make reservations.

Van's Place
Near Super Tubes
Bungalows
R $15

For other bookings: Call the *J-Bay Publicity Association.* Phone: 04321 93 2588

If you plan on staying in South Africa for any length of

time, check with *Shoreline Letting*, for help finding permanent lodging. Fax: 932-155.

Again, according to Hunt, there are lots of places to rent near Jeffrey's, but getting the ones near the water is difficult.

YMCA:
Phone: 011 403-3426
R $25 and up

YWCA:
Phone: 011 403-3830
R $32 and up.

Booking for hostels is available during peak season, November-February, and during school holidays. Booking fax number (27) 216-937. Some hostels provide meals for a price.

Camping is generally done in caravan parks, which are located throughout coastal and inland areas of South Africa. There are many other good camp sites operated by the National Parks Board. Contact them in Pretoria at: 643 Leyds St., Muckelenuck. Phone: 343-0930. In Capetown: Corner of Long and Hout. Phone: 22-2816. Sites available from R $10-R $25. They also have cottages available.

Johannesburg
Safari Caravan Park
Phone: 011 942-1404
R $20

Natal and Far North Coast
Umhlanga Caravan Park
Phone: 031 561-3217

Travskei
Saint John's
Municipal Caravan Park
Phone: 0475 44 1241
R $17.50
Flats from R $30

Cape Province
Palmiet Caravan Park
Phone: 02823 4050
R $20

Kogel Bay Pleasure Resort
Phone: 024 56 1286
R $12- R $25

Jeffrey's Bay Caravan Park
Phone: 04231 93111
Advanced booking on holidays
R $20

Cape Town and Peninsula
No need to book in advance except in holidays.

Sandvlei Caravan Park
Phone: 021 788 5215
R $11.50 (R $26.50 in peak season)

Fish hook Beach Caravan Park
021 782-5503
R $11 (R $25 in peak season)

Chapman's Peak Caravan Park
Phone: 021 789-1225
R $12.25

Municipal Caravan Park
Phone: 026-732 ask for 588
R $25

Saldanha Bay Caravan Park
Phone: 02281 42247
Tent Sites: R $20
Cottages: R $40-R $80

Strandfontein Municipal Caravan Park
Phone: 02723 51169
Camp sites: R $23
Chalets (Sleep 6) R $90

Cape Province-East Cape and Border
Sea Acres
Phone: 041 53-3095
R $12, plus R $5 additional person.

House sitting:
There is a charge of about R $8 a night (it's even less if
you plan on staying a month or more). To apply, contact: Mount Olive, Lindeshef Rd. Constantia Hills,
Phone: 780-0021

FOOD: Good food and almost all varieties. Excellent
Indian take-out food available.

Banks and post offices are common in the cities, and
keep the standard Monday through Friday hours.

MEDICAL CARE: Health standards are high, and city
water is drinkable. Avoid swimming in fresh water
which may be infected. Medicines are sold in pharmacies which keep regular hours in most major cities. Good
medical coverage is suggested, and visitors will be asked

to pay up front if they enter a hospital. Health requirements change, so check the latest information before traveling.

NATURAL HAZARDS: Some sharks beyond the population centers. Hippos and crocadiles near freshwater streams.

UNATURAL HAZARDS: It is ill advised to enter the townships without a guide. Car theft is prevelent within the big cities.

FURTHER ON: Some remote islands in the Indian Ocean have good surf. Also, much of Africa remains unexplored for surf potential. The major airports can take you anywhere in the world. Flights are going to be expensive. Check travel sections of major Sunday newspapers. Check the "Air Transportation" entry under "General Information" section in this book.

Dible

EUROPE

France

FIRST GLIMPSE: *Biarritz, France: Either "Surf Guide" or "Surfer Magazine." The caption was something about the place being the "Ala Moana of France." Apparently, the surf they photographed has since been destroyed by a jetty. When will they ever learn.*

BEST SEASON FOR SURF: Fortunately, the best season for surf is also the best season for weather: August-September.

SURFBOARDS: The surf can get big and powerful, a good semi-gun is recommend. Boards are sometimes sold by traveling surfers for a profit. The French seem to prefer boards with heavier glass jobs.

OTHER SURF ACCESSORIES: Short sleeve full-suit should suffice most of the time. Bring a good back-up leash, and anything else you'd bring if you were traveling the California coast.

WEATHER: Moderate July through September. By October the weather can turn cold, and stormy conditions become common.

AIR TRANSPORTATION:
Arrival: Charles de Gaulle Airport -
Phone: 48 62 22 80. Orly Airport - Phone: 48 85 5252

Paris Tourist Office:
127 au des Champs-E'lys
Phone: 47 2361 72

French Tourist Office: (310) 271-2358
General Information: (900) 990-0040

DOCUMENTS: European passport holders need only a valid passport. Nationals of other countries should contact their travel agents or their local French Consulate to obtain a visa application. For stays of longer than 90 days, you will need to apply for *"Carte de Se'jour.* Proof of income is required.

GROUND TRANSPORTATION: Rail is good and fast with *TGV* (Bordeaux, Nantes, Lyon, Lille, Marseille.) Other *SNCF* regular networks are efficient and serve main cities. The fast trains are *TGVs* or *Trains a Grande Vitesse.* Reservations are required. Slow trains are called *Autotrain.*

   If you're driving, get an International Driver's License. If you are hitching, try to look respectable and bring soft surf racks. Buses and trains take surfboards and are adequate for regional transportation. Taxis are reasonable. Check meters before entering. A 10 percent tip is expected.

Renting a car: Car rentals rates vary widely. Most of the major rental agencies are in evidence. A driver's license from the U.S., Canada or the U.K. is needed. An International Driver's License is a good idea. Rates drop if you book more than just a day at a time.

Alamo: (800) 327-9633
Avis: (800) 331-1212
Budget: (800) 527-0700
Hertz: (800) 654-3131
Cheaper rentals can be had from:
Auto Europe: (800) 223-5555
Europe by car: (800) 223-1516
Foremost Euro Car: (800) 272-3299

Leasing: 21 days or more offered by *Renault, Citroen, Pugeot* (in France) *Volkswagen, Ford, Audi* (in Belgium). Leasing is offered by *Europe by car* (800) 272-3299. Book car before you arrive.

If you are planing to travel in Europe for a month or more, you might be interested in **buying a cheap car** or a combi. Check around at the youth hostels. Some people buy new or nearly new German cars in Germany, drive them around Europe and sell them for a profit in the U.S., Australia, or other places where European cars are considered cool and cost a lot.

PETROL: Why do you think that most car chases take place on *Vespas* in European movies? Gas is too expensive for a *Trans Am*. About U.S. $3 per gallon.

Bicycles with surf racks or *Wheelies* might be a good option for those who are in good peddling shape. Mopeds are for hire in many areas, and are good for short distances.

CURRENCY EXCHANGE: One U.S. dollar = 4. 67 Francs. *Exchange rate will fluctuate.*

Money: To use a *Visa Card* in France a confidential PIN code is required. Check with your bank before traveling.

ELECTRICAL CURRENT: 220V, 50 cycles, AC

LODGING:
French Youth Hostel Association:
Phone: (33) (1) 448-98727
Fax: (33) (1) 448-98710

Hostels: There are more than 220 youth hostels in France. The following, except for one in Paris, are near the ocean.

Cap Ferret AJ Veret/ Country Hostel,
87 Avenue de Bourdeaux, 33970 Cap Ferret (Gironde).
Phone 566-06462

Concarneau
Quai de la Croix, BP
116, 29181 Concarneau Cedex (Finiste´re-Sud.)
Phone: 989-70347 Fax: 985-08757

Dieppe Offranville
48 Rue Louis Fromager, Quartiet Janval,
76550 Saint Aubin S/Scie (Seine-Maritime):
access Eglise de Janval/ Champs des Oiseaux.
Phone/fax: 358-48573

Dunkerque
Place Paul Asseman, 59140
Dunkerque (Nord): opposite the skating rink.
Phone: 286-33634 Fax: 286-32454

Fortenay-le Comte (Assoc)
Foyer sud Vendée "Les trois Portes",
16 Rue des Gravauts, BP 347, 85206
Fontenary-le-Comte.
Phone: 516-91344 Fax: 516-90443

Ile-de-Batz
AJ Verte/Country Hostel,
Auberge de Jeunesse/Ecole de Mer,
Créach Ar bolloc'h 29253 Ile-de Batz
(Finistére).
Phone: 984-19041 Fax: 986-17885

La Rochelle Centre
International de Séjour/ Auberges de Jeunesse,
Les Minimes, BP 305, 17013 La Rochelle Cedex
(Charente-maritime).
Phone: 464-44311 Fax: 464-54148

Paris
Cité des Sciences, 1 Rue Jean-Baptiste Clemente, 93310
le Pre' St Gervaus,
Phone: (1) 484-32411 Fax: (1) 484-32682

Plouguernevel (Assoc) AJ Verte/
Country Hostel, Centre de Vacances de Kermarc'h,
Plouguernevel, 22110 Rostrenen.
Phone: 962-91095

Quiberon
"Les Filets Bleus", 45 rue du Roch Priol,
56170 Quiberon (Morbihan).
Phone: 975-01554

Saint Brévin
"La Pinéde", All'ee de la Jeunesse, 44250 St-Brévin
(Lire Atlantique).
Phone: 402-72527 Fax: 406-44877

Trébeurden
Le Toeno, 22560 Trébeurden (Cotes-d'Armor).
Phone: 962-35222 Fax: 964-74434

Banking and post office--Normal Monday-Friday
hours.

FOOD: Most everything is good and safe to eat. Some
of the food might seem a bit rich.

PHONES: Country Code: (33). Main city codes: Paris:
(1). No city codes in other cities.

Health insurance is advised, but most hospitals will accept you in case of dire emergency.

POSTAL: Go to the PTT (post office) show a passport or other good ID. Expect to pay a small fee. Choose towns of size, to receive your mail if you're traveling. Mail can be picked up at the *American Express* office.

A FEW HELPFUL WORDS AND PHRASES: In France it is generally considered good manners to learn a bit of the language. English is quite common, but you'll want to know more than the following in some places.

yes—*oui*
no—*non*
please—*s'il vous plaît*
thank you—*merci*
good morning, good afternoon, hello—*bonjour*
goodbye—*au revoir*
good evening—*bonne noite*
shower—*douceh*
nights— *nuit*
Street—*rue*
tent—*tente*
youth hostel —*de la jeunesse*
petrol (gas)—*essence*
oil—*huile*
car—*voiture*
plane—*avion*
bread—*painr*
butterbeurre—*beurre*
table—*table*
yesterday—*hier*
now—*maintenant*
man—*un homme*
woman—*un femme*
glass—*verre*

fork—*fourchette*
knife—*coueau*
spoon—*cuiller*
salad—*salade*

NATURAL HAZARDS: Nothing major.

UNNATURAL HAZARDS: Not much in the way of localism. Big cities are typical in the ways of the theft and deception. Some bad water pollution near population centers.

PORTUGAL

FIRST GLIMPSE: *Surfer Magazine. Apparently the legendary board designer, Bob Simmons, studied maps and figured that Portugal had some of the best surf potential in the world.*

BEST SEASON FOR SURF: August-September

SURFBOARDS: Most everything will work, but you might want to bring something in the mid-seven-foot range if you are only bringing one board.

OTHER SURF ACCESSORIES: Bring everything from home—extra leash, a spring suit, rashguard, ding-repair kit.

DOCUMENTS: Visitors from most countries are not required a visa to visit Portugal if they plan on staying less than 60 days. Check before traveling.

GROUND TRANSPORTATION: Cars: Check entries in French section. Driving is on the right-hand side. Driving can be wild around town.

Trains: *Eurail* and *Inter-Rail* cards are valid but supplement must be paid on express trains. *RENFE*, offers a variety of discounts on tickets depending on the time of travel. *Eurail* and *Inter-Rail* cards are valid and subject to a supplement on some trains. **Buses** are adequate for some purposes, and offer special rates for those under 26 years old.

PETROL: About $4.20 per gallon.

LANGUAGE: Portuguese

CURRENCY EXCHANGE: One U.S. dollar = 134 Escudos. *Exchange rates will fluctuate.*

ELECTRICAL CURRENT: 220 V, 50 Cycles-AC

LODGING:
Hostels
Portuguese Youth Hostel Association
1000 Lisboa, Portugal
Phone: (351) (1) 355-9081 Fax: (351) (1) 352-8621

Areia Branca
Praia da Areia Branca, 2530 Lourinha
Phone: (61) 422-127 Fax: (61) 422-127
Cost: $1,150-$1,400

Fóz do Cávado
Pousada de Juventude de Fóz do Cávado, Fao Esposende, 4740 Esposende.
Phone/fax: (53) 981-793

Lisboa-Catalazete
Catalazete, estrada Marginal, 2780 Oeiras.
Phone/fax: (1) 4430638
Cost: $1,300-$1,700

Porto
Rua Rodrigues Lobo 98,4000 Porto.
Phone/fax: (2) 606-5535
Cost: $1,300-$1,400

Sintra
Pousada de Juventude de Sintra
St eufé mia, S. Pedro de Sintra,
2710 Sintra.
Phone/fax: (1) 924-1210
Cost: $1,150-1,400

MEDICAL CARE: Residential areas have adequate hospitals and clinics are open 24 hours a day for emergencies. The Farmacia' is where you buy medicines.

PHONES: Country Code (351). Main city codes: Faro (89). Lisbon (1) Porto (2).

A FEW USEFUL WORDS AND PHRASES:

breakfast—*pequeno almoco*
lunch—*almoco*
dinner—*jantar*
ford—*faca*
spoon— *colher*
cup— *xicana*
plate—*preto*
hello— *ola*
goodby—*adeus*
no—*nao*
good —*bom*

bad—*mau*
please—*fuz favor*
thank you—*obrigado*
day—*dia*
night—*norte*
water—*agua*
bread—*pao*
doctor—*medicio*
hospital—*hospital*
pharmacy—*farmicia*
bathroom—*cogsade bahno*
telephone—*telefone*
bank—*banco*

SPAIN

FIRST GLIMPSE: *When Peterson and Naughton first showed me photos of Mundaca in the early '70s, a perfect left point with a castle in the background, and nobody out, I went absolutely nuts with surf lust. Those early photos were overviews, but recent close-ups and water shots confirms the wave as a hefty barrel. Europeans are turning to surfing in droves these days, and many of the breaks made famous because they were great and uncrowded are now merely great. The waves are hot, and the living is easy if you know how.*

BEST SEASON FOR SURF: August-September

DOCUMENTS: Visas are required for residents of some counties. Check before departure.

CURRENCY EXCHANGES: One U.S. dollar = 116 peseta. *Exchange rates will fluctuate.*

ELECTRICAL CURRENT: 220 V, 50-cycle, AC

LODGING: Over 159 hostels to chose from, the following are on the coast. Those under 26-years-old get priority, the rats.

Hostels:
Aguadulce
"Aguadulce", Campillo del Moro s/n, 04720 Aguadulce, Almeria.
Phone: (950) 340-346 Fax: (950) 345-855
Make reservations early.

Aguilas-Calarreona Murcia.
Phone: (968) 413-029 Reservations at least seven days in advance.

Arriondas
"Arriondas", c/ Del Barco s/n,
Ariondas, Astruias.
Phone: (98) 584-0334

Cabera del mar
"Torre de Ametller", Veinat de Sta Elena d' Agell,
Cabrera del Mar, CP 08349 Barcelona:
Barcelona 30Km.
Phone: (93) 759-4448 Fax: (93) 750-0495
Reservations may be required.

Donostia-San Sebastian
"La Sirena", Igeldo Pasealekua 25,
Donostia, San Sebastian.
Phone: (943) 310-268, 311-293 Fax: (943) 214-090
Call or fax for reservations.

El Vendrell
"Sta Maria del Mar",
Av Palfuriana 80, 43880 Coma-ruga,

El Vendrell: Tarragona Phone: (977) 680-008
Fax: (977) 682-959
Call or fax above numbers, or
Phone: (93) 483-8363 Fax: (93) 483-8350 for reserva-
tions.

Luarca
"Fern'an Coronas", Villar s/n, Luarca, Asturias.
Phone: (98) 564-0676

Ma'laga
Plaza Pio XII 6, 29007 Ma'laga.
Phone/fax: (95) 230-8504

Madrid-Marcenado Calle Sta Cruz
de Marcenado No 28, Madrid.
Phone: (91) 547-4532

Moraira
AJ "La Marina" Camino Campamento 31,
03724 Moraira-Teulada, Alicante.
Phone: (96) 649-2030, 649-2044 Fax: (96) 649-1051
Call above numbers or, phone: (96) 389-252/ Fax: (96)
386-9951 for reservations.

Ribadesella
"Roberto Frasineli" c/ Ricardo Cangas s/n, la Playa,
Ribadeselaa, Asturias.
Phone: (98) 586-1380

Sada
"Marina Espanola, Corbeiroa, Bergondo,
Sada, La Coruna.
Phone: (981) 620-118
 Vigo

"Altamar" c/ Ces'areo Gonz'allez 4, CP
36210 Vigo CP, Ponteverda
Phone: (986) 290-808

A *Youth Hostel International Card* entitles you to a 30% discount on *KLM Royal Dutch Airlines* from Alicante, Barcelona, Madrid, Malaga and Palmas to Amsterdam, New York, Atlanta, Chicago, Houston, Los Angeles, Montreal, Toronto, Calgary and Vancouver, Mexico, Tokyo, New Delhi.

PHONES: International code (07) Country code (34) Main city area codes: Barcelona (3) Bilbao (4) Granada (58) Madrid (1) Sevilla (5) Valencia (6).

SURF CLUBS, ETCETERA

Surf clubs are often a good contact for the traveling surfer. They can provide tips about an area, sometimes a place to stay, and always a good party. The following is an incomplete list of clubs (mostly longboard-based). If you would like your club or organization listed in *The Surfer's Travel Guide*, please send the name, phone and address of your club to: *The Surfer's Travel Guide:* P.O. Box 697, Cardiff by the Sea, CA, USA 92007. We'll include the information in our next printing.

* Denotes member of Coalition of Surf Clubs.

*Pedro Point Surf Club
Contact: Danny Estella
P.O. Box 899 Pacifica, CA 94044
(415) 342-0215
Purpose: A community-based cultural organization dedicated to enjoying and improving ocean recreational opportunities and the coastal environment.

*Montara Fog Dogs
Contact: Greg Figeroa
1528 Rosita Rd.
Pacifica, CA 94044
Purpose: Friends, surf competitions, fun.

*Estero Bay Surf Club
Contact: Terry Swift
P.O. Box 25, Morro Bay, CA 93442
Purpose: To promote the sport of surfing with positive community action. Spreading goodwill while setting examples for and assisting the youth in our community.

*Santa Barbara Surf Club
Contact: Kenji Webb

P.O. 20137
Santa Barbara, CA 93120
(805) 962-5754
Purpose: Have fun, camaraderie, and set a good
example for our younger surfers.

*Malibu Boardriders Club
Contact: Kirby Kotler
28823 Cliffside Dr.
Malibu, CA 92065
(310) 457-4006
Purpose: A group of individuals born and raised in
Malibu who wish to surf, compete and have fun, but
most importantly, to give something back to surfing,
its community and the environment.

*Huntington Beach Longboard Crew
Contact: Eddie Enriquez
819 Governor St.
Costa Mesa, CA 92627
(714) 631-4494
Purpose: To encourage the evolution of high-perfor-
mance surfing with an emphasis on longboarding
while maintaining traditional surfing values and a
reverence for surfing history. To support groups and
activities which show concern for preserving and
maintaining the coastal environment.

*Blackie's Classics
Contact: Joe Catron
215 28th St.
Newport Beach, CA 92663
(714) 673-6057
Purpose: Fun, family-oriented. "We who love the
ocean and use it, want to keep it as long as we can."
Ask about the "Surf & Turf."

*San Onofre Surfing Club

Contact: Tom Metzger
P.O. Box 324
San Clemente, CA 92674
Purpose: To foster all phases of surfing, to make
responsible recommendations to the California Department of Parks and Recreation pertaining to the
operation and development of San Onofre Surfing
Beach, and to seek to retain the beach in its natural
state.

*Big Stick Surfing Association
Contact: Mike Young
539 Monterey Dr.
Aptos, CA 95003
(408) 688-7760
Purpose: In the spirit of Duke Kahanamoku, to promote friendship and camaraderie both in and out of
the water, so that surfing will thrive.
Note: Ask for information on the "Big Stick Classic."

*Doheny Longboard Surfing Club
Contact: Andy Cowell
P.O. Box 664,
Dana Point, CA 92629
(714) 494-7762
Purpose: Dedicated to the enjoyment of board surfing
in a clean and natural environment. To act as a
support group for other organizations with similar
views and objectives. Inquire about their annual club
contest.

*Swami's Surfing Association
Contact: Bruce King
1753 Wilstone Rd.
Encinitas, CA 92024
(619) 436-0638
Purpose: To promote the sport of surfing and fellow-
ship among surfers dedicated to the protection of

226

coastal resources and the creation of new surfing areas. Inquire about their annual club contest

*Santa Cruz Longboard Union
Contact: Ron Lindsay
430 Day Valley Rd.
Aptos, CA 95003
(408) 684-1551
Inquire about their memorial weekend club contest.

*Oceanside Longboard Surfing Club
Tara Lee Torburn
1115 Alberta
Oceanside, CA 92054
(619) 439-5334
Inquire about their annual club contest.

Association Of Surfing Professionals
Contact: Meg or Dory
P.O. Box 309
Huntington Beach, CA 92648
(714) 842-8826

Blue Water Task Force
Contact: Jim Reynolds
935 St. Albans Dr.
Encinitas, CA 92024

Dapper Dans
244 23rd St.
Manhattan Beach, CA 90266

Eastern Surfing Association
Contact: Kathy Phillips
New England District
126 Sayles Ave.
Pawtucket, R.I. 02860
(800) 937-4733

*Hawaiian Longboard Surfing Association
Contact: Bobby Kekoanui
P.O. Box 2147
Ewa Beach, CA 96706
(808) 949-4572
Purpose: To preserve the Hawaiian heritage.

*Hawaiian Surf Club
Contact: Jim Richey
3042 Shady Park Dr.
Long Beach, CA 90808-3923
(310) 832-0176

*Hole In The Wall
Contact: Brett Denholm
55 Tasman Rd.,
Avalon Beach, NSW, Australia 2107

International Surf Museum
411 Olive, Huntington Beach, CA 92648
Contact: Ann Beasley
(714) 960-3483

*Malibu Surfing Association
Contact: Gary Stellern
1460 Casa Grande, Pasadena, CA 91104
(818) 798-9868

Ohana Surf Club
Contact: Jeff Maxwell
2873 Peirpont Blvd.
Ventura, CA 93001

Old Man Longboard Club
P.O. Box 1795
Danville, CA
94526-6795

PLA
Contact: Rita
217 11th Street
Huntington Beach, CA 92648
(714) 960-7249

*Pacific Beach Surf Club
Contact: Glen Paculba
P.O. Box 99352
San Diego, CA 94044
(619) 273-7827

PSAA (Bud Surf Tour)
Contact: Ian Cairns/Alyisa Schwarzstein
P.O. Box 248
Laguna Beach, CA 92552

Sheboygen Longboard Surfing Association
Contact: Larry "Longboard" Williams
2010 South 10th St.
Sheboygen, WI, USA 53081

SIMA
Contact: Steve Helig
1555 Masonic Ave
San Franciso, CA 94117

South Florida Surfing Association
P.O. Box 292853
Davie, FL   33329

Surf Obsession
Contact: Robin Morris
42 Brickhill Rd.
Durbin, South Africa
Fax: 011 27 31 30 64 600

Surfers' Environmental Alliance
Contact: Steve Merrill
P.O. Box 3578
Santa Cruz, CA 95063

Surfrider Foundation
122 South El Camino Real
Suite # 67
San Clemente, CA 92672
(714) 492-8170

Surfing Walk Of Fame
P.O. Box 17
Huntington Beach, CA 92648

The British Columbia Surfing Association
Contact: Pete Enks
P.O. Box 79 Ucluelet, B.C. Canada
VOR 3AD

USSF (714) 493-2591

*Ventura Surf Club
Contact: Craig Angell
1480 Anita St.
Carpenteria, CA 93013
(805) 648-6711

Wind n' Sea Longboard Club
Box 134 La Jolla, CA 92038

Wollgoolga Longboard Club
Contact: Ted Quigley
P.O. Box 567
Woolgoolga, NSW, Australia 2456

*Bay Cities Surf Club
Contact: Richard Davidson
900 Palm Ave., Redondo Beach, CA 90278

British Longboard Association
SunGarth, British Road
St. Agnes, Cornwall, England
TR5 0TX

* Northwest Longboard Coalition
Contact: Al Pearly
P.O. Box 1904 Westport, WA 98595
(206) 268-0992

SURF CAMPS

Morris Overseas Tours
400 Ave. B, Melbourne Beach
Florida 32951
Phone: (800) 777-6853
They go to: Costa Rica, South Africa, Panama, Nicaragua, Barbados.
Tours for beginner through advanced.

The Surf Travel Company
P.O. Box 446
Cronulla, NSW 2230, NSW, Australia 2230
Phone 011-61-2-527-4722
They go to: Maldives, Tonga, Fiji, Western Samoa, Grajagan, Periscopes.
Tours for beginner through advanced.

Waterways Travel
Contact: Waterways Travel
1 15145, Calafia St. #1, Van Nuys, CA 91411
(800) 928-3757, (818) 376-0341
Fax: (818) 376-0353
Diving, fishing, surfing.
They go to: Costa Rica, Honduras, Mexico, Tahiti, Fiji, Samoa, Indonesia, Australia.

Easter Island
Easter Island Surf Cabanas
Contact: Carlos Lara, Arlegui 595 E-5
Vina Del Mar, Chile.
011-56-32-662574
Type of surf: intermediate to advanced

Tavarua Island Tours
Contact: Tavarua Island Tours, Inc.
 (805) 686-4551
Fax: (805) 683-6696

In the low season—December-February the cost is $125 per person per night.. $210 per couple per night. High season—March-November the cost is $135 per person. $230 per couple per night.

They arrange boat transportation, accommodations, meals and other activities.

Type of surf: Intermediate to advanced.

Samoan Surf Tours
Contact: Simon Schauble
P.O. Box 225 Apia, Western Samoa
Phone/Fax: 011-685-26377
They go to: Maninoa Surf Resort (Upolu Island) and Sevaii Surf Resort on Suvaii Island.
Type of surf: A variety of powerful reefs and points for beginner to advanced.

Fountain Of Youth Surf Adventures
Contact: Fountain Of Youth Surf Adventures
P.O. Box 933 Sunset Beach, CA 90742
Phone: (310) 592-1001
Season: March through October.
Seven to 17 day guided tours. Yacht charters available.
Price: $450 per week. Includes meals.
They go to: G'land, Uluwatu, Padang-Padang, Lombok, and Sumbawa.
Tours for intermediate through advanced surfers.

Baja Air Adventures,
991 Lomas Santa Fe Dr.,
Suite C221, Solana Beach, CA 92075
They go to: remote locations in Baja
Phone: (800) 221-9283. Fax: ((619) 259-8418
Air charter, includes food and camping gear.
$295 and up.
Tours for beginning through advanced surfers.

Baja Surf Adventures

Contact: Baja Surf Adventures
P.O. Box 1381 Vista, CA 92085
Phone: (800) 428-SURF
Fax: (619) 727-9868
They go to: various regions of Baja.
$200 and up.
Tours for beginning through advanced surfers.
Meals, and accommodations.

Todos Santos Tours
Contact: Todos Santos Tours
P.O. Box 2873
Newport Beach, CA 92659
(714) 721-8747
$200 per person on weekends.
Tours for intermediate to advanced surfers.

A Friend in Costa Rica
Contact: Chuck Herwig
5519 23rd St. East
Bradenton, FL 34203-4907
(813) 756-5867
Drug-free, eco-minded surfing adventures.
From $190 per week.
Tours for beginning to advanced surfers.
Handles surfboard repairs, rentals, cabanas available.

Surf Express
Contact: Carol Holland or Hunter Joslin
110 Polk Ave., # 4
Cape Canaveral, FL 32920
(407) 783-7814
$150 on up, depending upon the arrangements and package.
They go to: Costa Rica, Barbados, Nicaragua, Peru, Panama, Mexico.
Tours for Beginning through professional surfers.

Toucan Tours
P.O. Box 2755
Capistrano Beach, CA 92624
Phone/Fax: (714) 240-1959 or (800) 864-1099
They go to: both coasts of Costa Rica and other Central and South American countries.
Tours for beginning through professional surfers.

African Surf Tours
CC, A44 Rottingdean Court, 59 Rottingdean Rd.
Campus Bay 8001, South Africa
Phone 011-27-21-438-2386
Seasons: May to September
Guided tours
$100-$120 per day.
They go to: J-Bay and beyond.

RECOMMENDED BOOK LIST

"Hawaii Gets All The Breaks" by Greg Ambrose/ Bess Press, P.O. Box 22388, Honolulu, HI 96823

Living in Mexico: Send $12.95 plus $3 S&H to: *Living Easy in Mexico.* United Research Publishers, 103 North Highway 101, Dept. ADL-2, Encinitas, CA 92024.

Surfing and Sailboarding Guide to Australia, By Nat Young/ Palm Beach Press, 40 Ocean Rd., Palm Beach, NSW, Australia 2108

The Doctor's Book Of Home Remedies:, by the editors of *Prevention* Magazine Health Books/ Rodale Press, Book Reader Service, 33 East Minor St., Emmaus, PA 18098

Indo Surf & Lingo:, By Peter Neely

Surfing Guide To California, by Bank Wright

The Tico Times Guide
Apdo. 4632 San Jose, Costa Rica
U.S. residents send mail to: Dept. 717, P.O. Box, 025216, Miami, Florida 33102 U.S.A.

All Fodor's Guides

All Lonely Planet guides

The following books can be ordered through Magellan's Catalogue: Phone: (800) 962-4943 or write Box 5485, Santa Barbara, CA 93150-5485

The Safe Travel Book : #BB655, $12. 95

Travel Safe: #BB654, $7.95

Jet Smart: How to avoid the discomforts of air travel: #BB646, $12.95

Health on the Road: #BB649, $12.95

Airport Transit Guide: #BB643, $7.95

Pack It Up!: #BB653, $7.95

The Pocket Doctor #BB652V, $4.95

Phrase books:
Spanish : #BL651E, $ 4.95
French: #BL65IF, $4.95
Japanese: #BL651D, $4.95
Portuguese: #BL651P, $4.95

Magellan's Catalog: Box 5485, Santa Barbara, CA 93150-5485 U.S.A.

Anything from the American Automobile Association (AAA)

Hostelling International, *Budget Accommodation you can trust*
International Youth Hostel Federation
9 Guessens Road, Welwyn Garden City,
Herefordshire, AL8 6QW
England

South Pacific Handbook by Moon Publications, P.O. Box 1696-SF, Chico, CA 95927

Health Information for International Travelers. Call: (202) 783-3238.

The Baja Book

Mastering Business Etiquette and Protocol.
National Institute of Business Management
P.O. Box 1499, Alexandria, VA 22314

Anti Jet -Lag Diet. This is really a card, not a book. Send a self-addressed, stamped envelope to: Office of Public Affairs, P.O. Box 201, 9700 S. Cass Ave., Argonne, IL 60349.

American Express Traveler's Companion, P.O. Box 778883, Woodside, New York 11377.

To order the *Surfer's Travel Guide*, send $17.95, includes shipping and handling to P.O. Box 697-TG, Cardiff-by-the-Sea, CA 92007.

By the same author, *Good Things Love Water.* $17.95 includes shipping and handling. P.O. Box 697-W, Cardiff-by-the-Sea, CA 92007.

S hare a wave
and hoot
a kook.
—Skip Frye